Railway World

SPECIAL

THE SETT CARLISLE

Contents

Cover:
LMS '5' 4-6-0 No 5407 tops the summit at Ais Gill with the southbound 'Cumbrian Mountain Express' of 2 September 1981. *L. A. Nixon*

Right:
'Duchess' 4-6-2 No 46229 *Duchess of Hamilton* blasts away from Garsdale, after a photo-stop, with the southbound 'Cumbrian Mountain Express' of 11 February 1984. *W. A. Sharman*

Back cover, top:
No 92009 at Dent bound for Widnes.
Derek Cross

Back cover, bottom:
No 25.089 southbound at Ribblehead.
David A. Flitcroft

First published 1984
Reprinted 1985

ISBN 0 7110 1448 5

Published by Ian Allan Ltd, Shepperton, Surrey; and printed by Ian Allan Printing Ltd at their works at Coombelands in Runnymede, England

THE SETTLE & CARLISLE ROUTE

Introduction

ITS ADMIRERS are legion these days, but it is a fact that the Settle & Carlisle line was far from widely appreciated until the 1950s. Two photographers did much to evoke interest in the combination of wild, often gaunt scenery, noble civil engineering works and hard-worked steam locomotives. Those men were the late W. Hubert Foster (co-author of a memorable book on the line in the late 1940s) and the late Eric Treacy. In particular, Eric Treacy's work revealed the quintessential Settle & Carlisle steam railway scene, while *The Story of the Settle & Carlisle Line*, by Frederick W. Houghton & W. Hubert Foster, first published in 1948, recounted much of the lore of the line. Until the era of long-distance motorway journeys by car, and of course faster train journeys, the Settle & Carlisle was not largely appreciated at first hand.

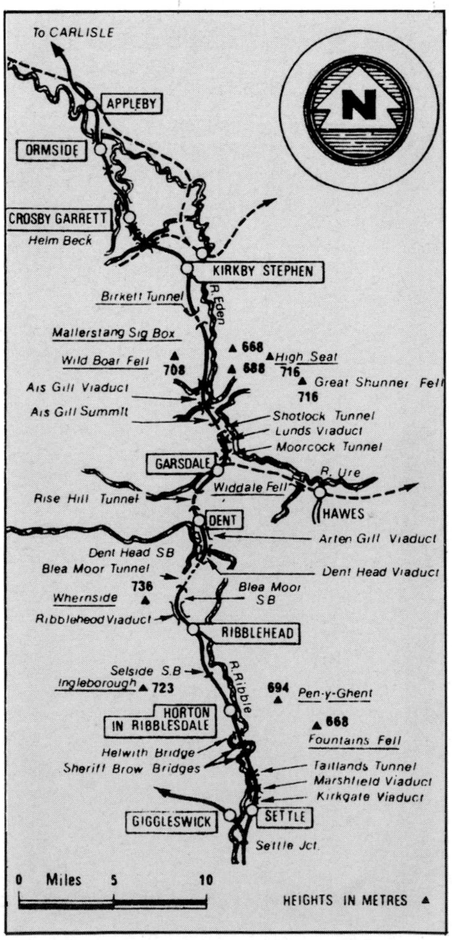

Only by walking the grand country is it possible to gauge the scale of the railway and concur with the view that the Settle & Carlisle is a great engineering achievement, not least because the style of the way and works is consistent, and the architectural and engineering work harmonious with the surrounding fells. Would that one could say the same of the M6 as it blunders through the Westmorland moorland and the Lune Gorge! The attraction also was that it was built as a main line for express trains, and made few concessions, as did early lines, for motive power of the pioneering days. But there were two other aspects, less appreciated. After World War 1, the passenger train service was always sparse, by the 1950s no more than three daytime and two night express trains each way. And in any case most of the services using it were through workings. Less obvious to the armchair reader was the fact that it was a ferociously hard section of line to work — in all seasons. Not for nothing was the Settle & Carlisle used for controlled road tests of locomotives, but the battle undertaken by men and machines against the capricious weather of the high fells was — and remains today — a contest with the elements.

This book is a celebration, not a requiem for the Settle & Carlisle and draws on material, mainly articles published in *Railway World* over the last 20 years, illustrated by courtesy of some noted photographers. Their content encompasses the construction of the line; the heyday of express services at the turn of the century; a unique account of the terrible winter of 1947; enginemanship in the latter days of the steam age; and concludes with an insight into the main line steam excursions of the late 1970s and early 1980s, featuring the career of George Gordon, a locomotive inspector at Carlisle, now retired.

Michael Harris
Editor

Above right:
Batty Moss viaduct — 'Patriot' 4-6-0 No 45506 *The Royal Pioneer Corps* crosses with a down goods, 11 April 1958. *I. S. Pearsall*

Right:
The northbound 'Cumbrian Mountain Pullman' of 27 March 1982 makes a rousing climb to Armathwaite viaduct behind 'King Arthur' 4-6-0 No 777 *Sir Lamiel* and LMS '5' 4-6-0 No 5407. *Tim Grimshaw*

L M S
5407
777

THE SETTLE & CARLISLE ROUTE

Renaissance of the Midland Railway

C. Hamilton Ellis

'What dreary country!' said the stout lady in the unbecoming striped costume.

The scene was a dining carriage of the Midland Railway, the place was near Blea Moor. Your author, then a small boy, had never in his life before travelled in so superb a train; he had only once before been on the Pennines, and he thought those vast, bare tops of England very grand indeed. But that was the first time the Striped Lady had made any comment on the scenery since leaving St Pancras, or had even looked out of the window. Neither the green shires nor the fiery stacks of Sheffield had stirred her. The same went for her idiotic children, who had only left off playing snap in order to fight, eat or to be led out feeling sick. Filled with a colossal sense of intellectual superiority, for I always despised people who were oppressed by solitude or made sick by trains, I reflected that the Stout Lady in Stripes would, without doubt, be everlastingly damned, and gave my attention back to the scenery and to the fleeting glimpses of our red engines pounding round the curves ahead. A horrid little boy I was, surely, but it was a most memorable journey.

It seems a very long time ago now, though of course it is not so in relation to Midland Railway history. The building of the Settle and Carlisle line, with its new route to Scotland, belongs to that great Midland Renaissance period, when Edward Shipley Ellis became chairman of the company and James Allport was general manager.

In the 1860s, the Midland Railway could count some Anglo-Scottish traffic, but could hardly boast about it. At Ingleton this had to be handed over to the London and North Western, and though the North Western, under such formidable worthies as Richard Moon and William Cawkwell, and now a very respectable railway, with its robbery-with-violence past decently unmentionable, it was still determined that companies like the Midland should know their place. Midland traffic sometimes took an incredible time to get from Ingleton to Carlisle. Midland passengers were attached to goods trains and dumped out on the bleak platforms at Tebay at ghastly hours. The Midland thought longingly of an independent route to the Border, and was backed up by the North British. An Act for the building of the Settle and Carlisle line was passed in 1865, giving the Midland use of Carlisle Citadel station. Then the Caledonian and the Glasgow and South

Western companies showed signs of wishing to amalgamate. As the Caledonian was an inseparable North Western ally, and as the Midland had been looking to the Sou-West for access to Glasgow, this was serious. The G&SWR had to be detached from its scandalous infatuation. By the time the necessary diplomatics had been achieved, the Midland was a little out-at-elbows. A great deal of money had been spent on the London extension, and the Scotch jackpot seemed more difficult to attain than ever. Now the North Western company craftily offered to talk turkey in regard to reviewing conditions of transfer traffic between Ingleton and Carlisle, on condition that the Midland abandoned its mad enterprise among the high fells. W. P. Price, then chairman of the Midland, faltered, and began to climb down. But he had reckoned without his allies, the North British, which looked forward to taking over remunerative traffic at Carlisle, and the Lancashire & Yorkshire, which would have a tap on the line in South Yorkshire, and be able to send its traffic straight to Scotland without dictation from the North Western. When the Midland sought to abandon its Settle and Carlisle project, it was firmly opposed by its friends, and the abandonment Bill was thrown out. The Midland seems to have pulled itself together with a sort of 'Heh-heh! Bless my buttons, what was I about? Even Jove nods, don't-you-know!' and, under the stern eyes of North British and L&Y proceeded to carry out its duty.

Out of Tasmania, that remote island a little like an Antipodean Scotland, where

Left:
The grandeur of the prospect at Batty Moss, Ribblehead, looking towards the viaduct which is being crossed by the up 'Thames-Clyde Express' in June 1969. *C. T. Gifford*

Above:
The awesome prospect of the northern portal of the 2,629yd Blea Moor Tunnel, as seen from an LMS '5' 4-6-0. *Paul Riley*

Centre right:
A view from Dentdale, with Arten Gill Viaduct being crossed by the down 'Waverley' behind 'Jubilee' 4-6-0 No 45694 *Bellerophon* in April 1958. *I. S. Pearsall*

Bottom right:
Garsdale by night, Easter 1983. *T. G. Flinders*

Right:
Sometimes forgotten as a part of the Settle & Carlisle — the now-closed Hawes branch. This was the scene on Whit Saturday 1954, showing the typical S&C style station, looking towards Northallerton. Class '2' 2-6-2T No 41206 has brought in the 12.45pm from Bradford Forster Square. *G. B. Blacklock*

Below right:
The scene as the railway runs on a ledge above Dentdale. Arten Gill Viaduct is in the background, and the unusual train consists of North British Railway 'C' 0-6-0 No 673 *Maude* and Caledonian Railway coaches steaming through heavy rain on their return to Falkirk from Rainhill and Rocket 150, 31 May 1980.
T. G. Flinders

there were marsupial wolves and other improbable creatures, but no railways before 1871, came a huge pioneer named Sharland. He it was who surveyed the Settle and Carlisle line, and planned it with a ruling gradient of 1 in 100. The Midland Railway got that ruling gradient, but they got over 20 miles of it. Over the fells he went, this gaunt young engineer from the south of the world. One of his bases was the Gearstones Inn, 11 miles up from Settle and many more from anywhere else, and there, in the course of his survey, he was snowbound for three weeks.

So he plotted his line, and so it was built, through the carboniferous limestone of the North West Riding, by Pen-y-Ghent, and the table-mountains of Ingleborough and Wild Boar Fell, through the boulder clay, which slides about when wet and sets like concrete when dry, by tunnel and great viaduct, and across the great Pennine Fault into the Permian beds and the more luscious Vale of Eden. The big man conquered the fells, and in conquering he died.

In the path which he had blazed there sprang up the navvy towns. Where Ribble gushes from the limestone (we call it Ribblehead today, and for many years since), there was Batty Green, taking its name from a pothole with the engaging name of Batty Wife's Hole. It should be added that the name had a frightful origin, connected with the end of the late Mrs Batty. It had a population of over 2,000, a schoolmaster to teach the wild children of wilder men and women, a parson who waded through the mire, gaitered like a bishop. It had Sunday fights galore. Its beef arrived on the hoof. Its architecture consisted of appalling hovels. There were other, lesser places (though two supported schoolmistresses, and one wonders what manner of tough Victorian girls they were!), and where they were is now nothing but huge, bare hills, rock outcrops, short sere grass and a most noble railway. The work was carried out under five contracts, including one for the six-mile branch from Hawes Junction to Hawes. Resident engineers and navvies worked in isolation, building towards each other. There was Blea Moor tunnel (2,629yd long), through millstone grit, limestone and shale, its summit 1,151ft above ordnance datum and the crown of its arch 500ft below the moor, at the end of a 12-mile climb and a rise of 700ft from Settle. Headings were driven from seven shafts, so that there were 16 working faces at once. Rock drilling was not

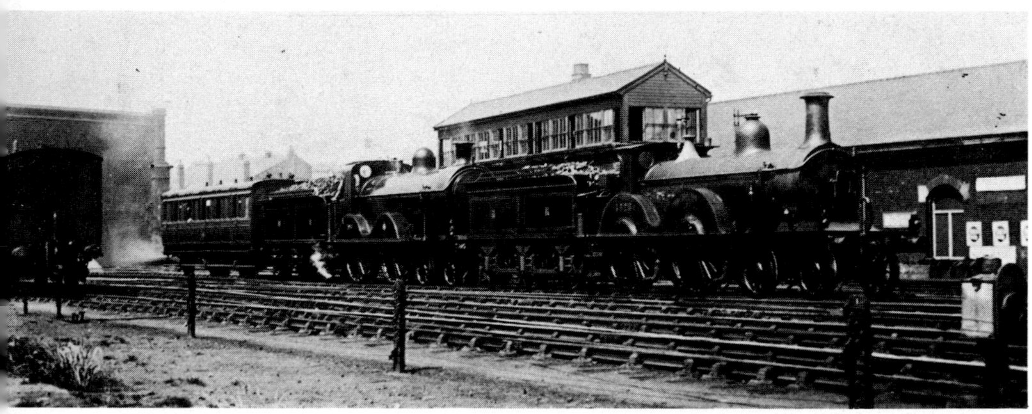

Above:
The scene at the south end of Carlisle Citadel station. The locomotives are Midland Railway 4-4-0s, 1877-built No 1328 leading with No 196 of 1894, reboilered 1905 behind. They will attach the North British Railway saloon to a southbound S&C express. *LPC/Ian Allan Library*

Below:
In early LMS days, LMS Compound 4-4-0 No 1071 drops down towards London Road Junction, having left Carlisle Citadel with a southbound express routed over the Settle & Carlisle.
H. Gordon Tidey/Ian Allan Library

advanced in the early 1870s. Lighting was by candles which, like old-time miners, the men carried on their caps.

The building of Blea Moor tunnel took over four years. It proved a damp, terrible tunnel. It drove men mad, so that they could go underground no more. To this day, though much shorter than many English tunnels, it is a horrible place. Freaks of temperature prevent the smoke from escaping up the shafts in certain weather. The rain trickles down the shafts; in winter it freezes on its way down; the austerely pure icicle becomes an obscene black *bougie* depending with hundreds of others in each monstrous vent.

But what is a mile and a half of Styx in 70 miles of the Delectable Mountains? The experience of travel, in fair or foul times, from Hellifield by Settle to Carlisle, on plush or on footplate, would be the poorer without Blea Moor tunnel, though none but a blockhead would walk through it for fun. Nor are those Delectable Mountains any place for elegant promenading. They are no more for the sissy-aesthete than they were for the Stout Lady in Stripes. They are the backbone of England.

Construction began in November 1869, and the first sod was cut near Settle, in the policies of Anley House. Estimated cost of the line was £2,200,000. In fact, it came to £3½million. J. S. Crossley was resident engineer during building. Winter and summer the navvies toiled, under that heat that can come where huge hills close in, lashed by those winter winds that only the Pennines know. English, Irish and Scots were there, and when they were not working they bashed each other with the bare fist. In each community there was a Cock o' t' Camp; he owed his title to his knuckles, and kept it until one of his numerous challengers defeated him. In the early summer of May 1871, smallpox broke out, and did far more terrible damage than any Sunday morning blood-bath. At and around Batty Green, during the years 1869-76, nearly a hundred died through accident, sickness and explosure to the weather.

It is tempting to go on writing of the Settle and Carlisle line through many pages, but fortunately there are already numerous excellent histories of it already written, plagiarism of which would be difficult to avoid. In 1873, coal traffic was being handled as far as Dent Head. On 2 August 1875, goods trains began running between Settle and Carlisle. During the autumn and winter, special rolling stock for the new Scotch expresses was being built, and passenger trains began running from St Pancras to Glasgow St Enoch, and Edinburgh Waverley, via Settle and Carlisle, on 1 May 1876. The new line began at Settle Junction, on the 'Little' North Western line, and ended at Petteril Bridge Junction on the Newcastle and Carlisle line of the North Eastern Railway. Thus, the newest main line in the north of England was linked to the oldest, the Newcastle and Carlisle Railway having been completed in 1839. Many years after, this resulted in LMS expresses from the south entering Carlisle over the LNER.

Today the line stands as it did; it has grown into the country, and into the lives of the people. In these days, these high days of the motor, the Midland main line remains a life-giving artery for communities in remote places. From Settle Junction to Petteril Bridge is rather more than 72 miles. The climb begins in the first mile; between Settle Junction and Blea Moor tunnel it rises at 1 in 100 for nearly 10½ out of 15 miles, ending in the tunnel itself. Beyond Blea Moor, the line is easier, but still rising, with a short stretch at 1 in 120, to the summit level of 1,169ft at Ais Gill signalbox. In Blea Moor tunnel itself, as already remarked, is a summit of 1,151ft. Dent, at 1,145ft, is the highest railway station on an English main line. From Ais Gill the descent to near sea-level at Carlisle is longer than the ascent from Settle, but in its 47 miles it includes nearly 12 miles on 1 in 100, accounted for by most of the stretch from the summit to Ormside viaduct.

Heavy engineering works abound. Ribblehead viaduct, built of the surrounding limestone, has 24 spans, a length of 440yd, and a maximum height of 165ft above valley bottom. Every sixth pier is 18ft thick at the spring of the arch, and the others are 6ft thick. It took five years to build. Smardale viaduct is 237yd long and 130ft high, with 12 spans. This also occupied five years in building. The last stone was laid in 1875 by Mrs Crossley, wife of the resident engineer. The foundations go down to 45ft below the riverbed of Scandal Beck. Moorcock viaduct stands across the bog called Dandry Mire, where a high embankment was originally intended but proved impossible. It is 227yd long and 50ft high, with 12 spans. Ormside viaduct provides the first crossing of the River Eden, and gives the traveller a view of great loveliness after the savage country through which he has passed from the south. It is 200yd long and 90ft high, with 10 spans. The second crossing of the Eden is on Long Meg viaduct, a beautiful thing of the local red sandstone.

Other viaducts, many of them over 100yd long, are the two Ribble viaducts south of Ribblehead, Dent Head, Arten Gill, Lunds, Ais Gill (just over the watershed, 1,167ft above sea-level), Crosby Garrett, Griseburn, Long Marton, Crowdundle (on the Westmorland-Cumberland County March), Dodd's Mill (Little Salkeld), Armathwaite, Dry Beck and High Stand Gill. Griseburn viaduct marks the halfway stage between Settle and Carlisle.

There are over 3¼miles of tunnel, though only Blea Moor exceeds a mile between portals, with its 2,629yd. The next longest is Rise Hill (1,213yd). Other tunnels are, in order going north, Moorcock, Shotlock Hill, Birkett, Crosby Garrett, Helm, Culgaith, Waste Bank, Lazonby, Baron Wood Nos 1 and 2, and Armathwaite. Of these, Birkett tunnel (424yd long) is interesting in that it occurs on the great geological fault of the Pennine Chain, and was bored through a remarkable succession of shale, magnesium and mountain limestone, millstone grit, slate, iron-ore, coal and lead.

Left:
The gently undulating uplands south of Kirkby Stephen are traversed by Brush/Sulzer Co-Co diesel No D1860 at the head of a diverted Glasgow-Birmingham express on 29 April 1967. *John M. Boyes*

The Midland train services of 1905

C. J. Allen

In the middle of the first decade of the 20th century the Midland Railway was at the zenith of its influence and prestige. Its total route mileage of 1,848 was exceeded only by the 3,025 miles of the GWR and the 2,063 miles of the LNWR, though its total single track mileage of running lines and sidings — 5,974 — was greater than the North Western's 5,770 miles. In the area of country that it covered longitudinally it had no superior, with its 317-mile main line from Bristol via Birmingham, Derby, Chesterfield and Rotherham to Leeds and Carlisle. Its joint ownership of the Somerset & Dorset Joint Line extended its orbit through to the southern coast, at Bournemouth; to the east its share in the Midland & Great Northern Joint Railway took its trains as far as Yarmouth; in the west by the use of running powers it reached a line of its own extending into Swansea; and from its northern extremity at Carlisle its partnership with the G&SWR found M&GSW coaches — of standard Midland design — in the St Enoch station at Glasgow, while similar 'M&NB' coaches and sleeping cars penetrated much further north, to Aberdeen, Inverness and Fort William.

Some of this joint coaching stock also achieved record daily mileages. For example, the 7.55pm from Bristol conveyed through coaches for both Glasgow and Aberdeen, the latter covering a distance of 546 miles nightly. But this was beaten by the 573 miles travelled by the through coaches from St Pancras to Inverness and the even longer 577 miles in summer of the through St Pancras-Fort William coach. As we shall see later, through coach workings in many directions were a feature of Midland operation, all of which had to be conducted in highly competitive conditions. Between London and Scotland the Midland suffered by longer distances and more severe gradients in its competition with the East and West Coast routes, but not a few travellers used the Midland because of the superior comfort of its rolling stock; and then, of course, there was the fact that important cities like Leicester, Nottingham, Sheffield and Leeds were on its principal main line, and thus were provided with through communication to and from Scotland.

Between St Pancras and Manchester the Midland put up a magnificent fight with the LNWR closely paralleling the latter's times depite the tremendous climb to Peak Forest summit. As to the traffic between London, Leicester, Nottingham and Sheffield the Great Central had now become a formidable competitor, while between London, Leeds and Bradford the Great Northern was able to achieve faster times. Then between the west of England and Manchester, Liverpool and Scotland, the Midland competed with the Great Western and London & North Western Severn Tunnel route, and also between Birmingham and the same areas with the LNWR.

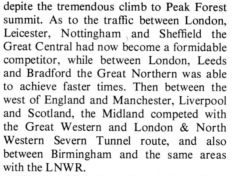

Above:
One of the 2606-10 series 4-4-0s, built at Derby in 1900, at Hawes Junction (later Garsdale) with an up Anglo-Scottish express. Note the local train set for the Northallerton line in the bay platform. *Ian Allan Library*

Above right:
The Deeley '999' 4-4-0s were built especially for Settle & Carlisle line service. No 997, the third in the class, approaches Carlisle Citadel with a down Anglo-Scottish express.
Ian Allan Library

Below right:
Midland Compound 4-4-0 No 1010 (formerly No 1005 and so numbered until 1907) sets out from Carlisle Citadel with an up express over the Settle & Carlisle. *LPC/Ian Allan Library*

The use of light formations had permitted the Midland to build up one of the fastest train services in the country, and for this early period many of the timings were brilliant indeed. Like the light trains, so the Midland Railway throughout its independent history never built anything more powerful than 4-4-0 locomotives for passenger service nor 0-6-0s for freight; but this resulted in more double-heading of trains than on any other British railways. As to locomotive power, S. W. Johnson had introduced in 1902 his first two three-cylinder compound 4-4-0s, Nos 2631 and 2632, most imposing machines for the period, and very soon in the news because of their outstanding performances. The *Locomotive Magazine* of October 1902, for example, recorded that on a day in September, No 2631 had worked the 1.30pm Scotch express out of St Pancras from Hellifield to Carlisle, $76\frac{3}{4}$ miles, in 79min, climbing the initial 17.2 miles to Blea Moor in $24\frac{1}{4}$min, averaging 69mph from Ais Gill down to Carlisle, and picking up 13min of a late start; this was with a load of equal $13\frac{1}{2}$ or about 210 tons. On the fastest timings the compounds were allowed to take up to 240 tare tons.

We come now to the timetables themselves, and first, to the Anglo-Scottish services from and to St Pancras. The day began with the 9.30am down, first stop Leicester (99.1 miles in 113min), next Chesterfield (and here, strange to relate, with a wait of no less than 54min for a connection to Sheffield), after which the direct line was taken to Rotherham and the next stop was Leeds, at 1.23pm. Between Leeds and Carlisle the only stop was at Hellifield, and the border city was reached at 3.45pm. The

4968

1010
1010

Left:
Midland Railway 4-4-0 No 463 (a '483' class renewal of an 1894-built locomotive) heads out of Carlisle towards Petteril Bridge Junction with an express for St Pancras.
H. Gordon Tidey/Ian Allan Library

Below:
One class associated with the Settle & Carlisle was the '800' class 2-4-0s, built from 1870. This is No 813A, in the 1902-07 period, and seen outside Carlisle Citadel. Sister engine No 815 (by then No 48) was destroyed in the Hawes Junction accident of December 1910.
Locomotive & General Railway Photographs (8031) Courtesy David & Charles

Right:
The Midland's Carlisle Durran Hill running shed served the Settle & Carlisle line. This view shows a selection of locomotives including 0-6-0s and an 0-6-0T, with 4-4-0 No 1813 in the foreground. *Ian Allan Library*

Glasgow portion of the train, with the restaurant cars, was into that city by 6.25pm; passengers for Edinburgh were provided with their own restaurant car onwards from Carlisle and were run non-stop by the North British to the Scottish capital in $2\frac{1}{4}$hr, arriving at 6.5pm. This section included through coaches for both Aberdeen and Perth. While it may be admitted that under nationalisation London-Edinburgh traffic is concentrated on the East Coast Route, it is astonishing to have to add that the timing of 9hr 25min by the 10.15am from St Pancras to Edinburgh on the winter service, after a lapse of 60 years, is 50min slower than the 8hr 35min of 1905.

After the 9.30am came the 11.30am, also to Glasgow and Edinburgh, with a conditional stop at Luton to pick up, then Leicester, and after that a non-stop run to Leeds, reached at 3.22pm. This train divided at Hellifield; the Glasgow portion, having acquired through coaches from Liverpool and Manchester via Blackburn, was first away, non-stop to Carlisle (5.50pm) and into Glasgow by 8.25pm; the Edinburgh portion, like that of the 9.30am down having attached its own restaurant cars, stopped at Appleby and various Scottish stations and reached Edinburgh at 8.37pm. Last of the day trains from London was the 1.30pm, calling at Leicester, then Sheffield (4.39pm), Leeds (5.30pm) and Hellifield to Carlisle (7.55pm).

The G&SWR gave this express such a smart run on to Glasgow that its arrival at St Enoch at 10.20pm tied with the Central station arrival of the 2pm Corridor from Euston, which left Carlisle 13min later but used a route 13 miles shorter.

It is a damaging reflection on our modern service that whereas in 1905 it was possible to leave Sheffield as late as 4.43pm and Leeds at 5.36pm in a through express for Glasgow, the latest through train departures to Glasgow from these cities are at 1.20 and 2.40pm respectively. There can be later starts from both Sheffield and Leeds either via York or Manchester, but involving changes, times nothing like as fast, and extra cost because of the considerably increased mileage.

The down Midland night service in 1905 also was notable. Sufficient store was set by the Stranraer-Larne route to Northern Ireland for the Midland to provide a very fast train from St Pancras at 8.30pm with a run to Leicester in 105min, and a Sheffield arrival in 3hr flat (such a train today would be greatly appreciated by Leicester, and possibly by Sheffield also); Leeds was reached at 12.22am and Carlisle at 2.45am, the $6\frac{1}{4}$hr timing to this point tieing with that of the 9.30am down. This train also conveyed a Glasgow portion, arriving at 6.10am.

The principal night Glasgow train, however, was the 12 midnight down, calling only at Leicester and Trent to Leeds (4.00am), and non-stop from there to Carlisle (6.23am) where even at this early date the G&SWR helped to boost the Midland route by attaching a breakfast car; Glasgow was reached at 9am. Between the 8.30pm and 12 midnight was the 9.30pm calling at Bedford and Nottingham (11.55pm-12.0 midnight) and then making the only non-stop run of the day from Nottingham to Leeds. Here the Glasgow and Edinburgh portions separated, taking on with them the through coaches already mentioned off the 7.25pm from Bristol. The Edinburgh portion left Leeds first, at 1.50am, reaching the Scottish capital at 6.45am, while the Glasgow portion, at 2.0am, was into St Enoch at 7.5am.

By comparison with the two day and two night express trains between Hellifield and Carlisle today which are the only ones still remaining, it is amazing to recall that in 1905 the Midland was running six day and four night expresses over this line in each direction daily. In the morning there were the 9.30am from Liverpool Exchange and 9.35am from Manchester Victoria, worked by Midland locomotives throughout to Blackburn and from there as one train to

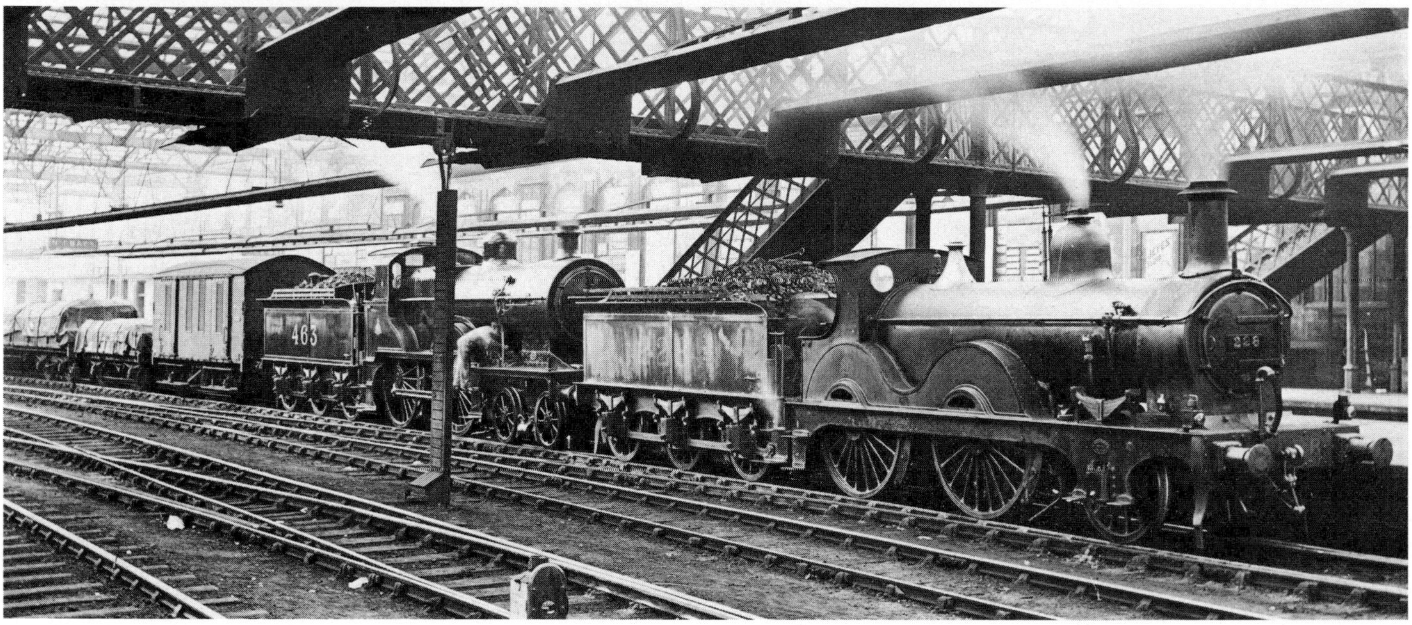

Above:
An up theatrical special rests in Carlisle Citadel headed by '1400' class 2-4-0, with its post-1907 number of 228, leading '483' rebuilt 4-4-0 No 463 in final Midland Railway days.
Ian Allan Library

Hellifield, where they divided into separate Glasgow (11.0am) and Edinburgh (11.16am) trains, each having attached through coaches which had left Leeds at 10.0am. Following these were the 9.30am and 1.30pm and the two portions of the 11.30am from St Pancras, with the night 8.30pm, 9.30pm (two portions) and 12.0 midnight from St Pancras.

Southbound, the counterpart of the 9.30am from St Pancras was the 9.20am from Glasgow, attaching at Carlisle through coaches off the 9.30am from Edinburgh. This train was unique in that its only stop between Carlisle and Leeds was at Hawes Junction (the modern Garsdale) where a through coach for Manchester was detached, to be taken forward by the 10.55am 'slow' from Carlisle, which was overtaken at this lonely and lofty junction by the Scottish train. This was the fastest train of the day up from Leeds; it missed both Sheffield and Leicester and called only at Trent (where a through coach for Nottingham was detached and replaced by a slip coach for Kettering), and London was reached at 6.15pm. Next, the 10.30am from Edinburgh and the 11.0am from Glasgow ran separately (calling only at Hellifield) as far as Leeds, where they were combined to leave at 4.2pm for a fast run to St Pancras, calling only at Sheffield and Leicester and arriving at 8.5pm; a through coach from Glasgow to Bristol ran as far as Sheffield in this train, which also acquired at Leeds a through coach from Barrow-in-Furness. The afternoon expresses from Glasgow and Edinburgh, however, ran independently throughout to London. The 1.30pm from Glasgow, having collected at Leeds a through coach from Harrogate, left there at 6.22pm and Sheffield at 7.12pm for Nottingham, from which a very fast run was made over the 123.5 miles to St Pancras (including a conditional stop to set down at Luton) in 132min, at 56.1mph. The Edinburgh express afforded passengers from that city a start as late as 2.15pm, and was not away from Carlisle till 4.45pm nor from Leeds till 7.17pm; the stops after that were at Masborough (Rotherham), Trent and Leicester only and St Pancras was reached at 11.15pm.

The night trains were not quite as fast as those in the down direction; the 9.30pm from Glasgow and 9.50pm from Edinburgh, both with sleeping cars, combined with the Stranraer train to make the run up from Leeds with only one intermediate stop, at Leicester, arriving at 7.10am; there was also the 11.0pm sleeper from both the Scottish cities, calling after Leeds at Sheffield and Trent, and due at 8.0am, with a smart run up from Trent in 135min.

The summer 1903 timetables

Above:
Lineside photographers alongside the Settle & Carlisle were rare in pre-Grouping days which accounts for the preponderance of Carlisle views of S&C trains. 4-4-0 No 82, as rebuilt in 1904, leaves Carlisle with a local train, including a saloon behind the engine.
Locomotive & General Railway Photographs (8026) courtesy David & Charles

Right:
The handsome lines of '999' 4-4-0 No 998 are seen to advantage as it takes a southbound express away from the North Western main line at Carlisle. Note the 12-wheel dining carriage second in the train. *H. Gordon Tidey*

Far right and overleaf:
Timetable extracts from the Midland Railway public timetables dated July-September 1903.

PRINCIPAL EXPRESS SERVICES.

ENGLAND AND SCOTLAND,

VIA SETTLE AND CARLISLE,

Valley of the Eden, Land of Burns, Home & Haunts of Scott, Forth Bridge, &c.

TO SCOTLAND.—WEEKDAYS. / SUNDAYS.

	Weekdays											Sundays			
		Luncheon cars London to Edinburgh and dining cars Edinburgh to Aberdeen	Luncheon cars London to Glasgow	Dining cars London to Glasgow	Dining cars London to Edinburgh	Dining cars London to Glasgow	Sleeping car London to Edinburgh, Perth and Inverness. Saturday nights and Sunday mornings excepted. Dining and supper cars London to Leeds	Sleeping car London to Stranraer Harbour. Saturday nights and Sunday mornings excepted.	Dining and supper cars London to Leeds. Sleeping car London to Edinburgh	Sleeping car London to Glasgow	Sleeping car London to Glasgow. Breakfast car Carlisle to Glasgow (Sundays excepted.)	Sleeping car London to Stranraer Harbour	Sleeping car London to Edinburgh	Sleeping car London to Glasgow	Sleeping car London to Glasgow. Breakfast car Carlisle to Glasgow
LONDON (ST. PANCRAS) dep.	5 15	9 30	9 35	11 30	11 35	1 30	7 30	8 30	9 30	9 30	12 0	8 30	9 30	9 30	12 0
LEICESTER .. .. ,,	7 20	11 28	11 28	1 30	1 30	3 27	8 54	10 30	10 35	10 35	2 0	10 30	10 30	10 30	2 0
NOTTINGHAM ,,	7 35	11 5	12 0	1 0	2 2	2 51	9 19	9 19	12 0	12 0	2 0	.....	12 0	12 0	2 0
PLYMOUTH .. .. .. ,,	8G20	..	..	..	..	8 30	2 15	2 15	3A50	3A50	..	..	2 10	2 10	..
BRISTOL ,,	1D 3	.....	.....	9 45	9 45	12 20	6 5	6 5	7 55	7 55	8 15	.....	7 55	7 55	.....
CARDIFF .. .. .. ,,	10M39	..	..	8 0	8 0	10 20	4 25	4 25	6 8	6 8	..	..	3 36	3 36	..
BIRMINGHAM ,,	4D 8	10 12	10 12	11 50	11 50	2 25	8 20	8 20	10 33	10 33	11 25	.....	10 33	10 33	11 25
DERBY .. .. ,,	7 2	11 30	11 30	12 57	12 57	3 32	9 5	9 5	11 37	11 37	12 55	..	11 37	11 37	12 55
SHEFFIELD ,,	9 0	12 13	1 3	2 5	2 12	4 2	9 32	11 49	12 35	12 35	1 58	11 49	12 35	12 35	1 58
LEEDS .. .. ,,	10 0	1 28	1 28	3 28	3 28	5 33	11 23	12 42	1 50	2 0	4 5	12 42	1 50	2 0	4 5
BRADFORD ,,	9 42	12B50	1 20	2 40	2 40	5 5	10B 0	10B50	1 20	1 20	2B 5	10B25	1 20	1 20	2B 5
LIVERPOOL (Exchange) .. ,,	9 30	12 35	12 35	2 20	2 20	4 35	..	..	12 45	12 45	..	.....	12 45	12 45	..
MANCHESTER (Victoria) .. ,,	9 35	12 30	12 30	2 25	2 25	4 40	.....	.....	12 50	12 50	.....	..	12 50	12 50	.....
CARLISLE .. .. .. arr.	12 35	3 45	4 5	5 50	6 0	7 55	1 30	2 55	4 15	4 30	6 25	2 55	4 15	4 30	6 25
AYR ,,	3 54	....	6 51	8 41	..	10 43	..	5 51	....	7E28	9 25	5 51	.....	7 28	9 25
GLASGOW (St. Enoch) .. ,,	3 20	..	6 35	8 25	..	10 20	....	6 10	..	7E 5	9 0	6 10	..	7 5	9 0
GREENOCK ,,	4 37	....	8 2	9 52	....	12 5	..	7 26	....	8 42	10 20	7 26	.....	8 42	10 20
EDINBURGH (Waverley) ,,	3 30	6 5	..		8 35	10 25	3 50		6 45		12L 5	..	6 45	..	12 5
OBAN .. ,,	9 5	....	....		4L45		11 55		11L55		6L30	.....	11 55	.....	6 30
FORT WILLIAM .. .. ,,	9I38	..	..		..		9 43		12L28		9L36	..	12 28	..	9 38
MALLAIG ,,	....	....	....		....		11 32		7P30		....	....	7 30	....	....
DUNDEE ,,	6 15	8 10	....		10 51		5 28		9E 5		3L37	....	9 5	....	3 37
ABERDEEN .. .. ,,	8 40	10 5	..		12 50		7 20		11E10		6L 0	..	11 10	..	6 0
PERTH ,,	6 20	7 52	....		10 36		5 5		8 55		3L 5	....	8 55	....	3 5
INVERNESS .. .. ,,	..	12 10	..		5L10		9 10		1 50	..	8L35	..	1 50	..	8 35

Sundays, last column, Carlisle to Perth: Arrivals on Mondays.

FROM SCOTLAND.—WEEKDAYS. / SUNDAYS.

	Weekdays														Sundays	
	Luncheon cars Carlisle to London	Luncheon cars Glasgow to London	Dining cars Edinburgh to London	Dining cars Glasgow to London	Dining cars Glasgow to London	Dining cars Edinburgh to London			Tea car Glasgow to Carlisle		Sleeping car Glasgow to London	Sleeping car Edinburgh to London		Saturday nights and Sunday mornings excepted. Sleeping cars Glasgow, Inverness, Perth, and Edinburgh to London	Sleeping car Glasgow to London	Sleeping car Edinburgh to London
INVERNESS dep.	10M30	....	....			8 40	....	....		11 10		3 50	3 50	5 30	.....	10 10
PERTH ,,	6 30	..	8 35			12 30	..	..		4 10		7 55	7 55	9 40	..	4 10
ABERDEEN .. .. ,,	....	....	6 20			10 20	....	....		1 25		5 30	5 30	7 45	.....	3 30
DUNDEE .. .. ,,	6 40	..	8 10			12 20	..	..		3 35		7 30	7 30	9 35	..	5 30
MALLAIG ,,	....	....	....			6 25	....	....		....		1 15	1 15	2 15	.....	.....
FORT WILLIAM .. ,,	..	..	..			8 25	..	..		..		3 20	3 20	4 20	..	..
OBAN ,,	....	....	....			7 45	....	....		12 40		4 15	4 15	4 15	.....	.....
EDINBURGH (Waverley) ,,	9 30	..	10 30			2 15	..	2 35		6 0		10 0	10 15	11 30	..	9 30
GREENOCK ,,	..	8 25	....	10 0	12 30	....	1 10	....	4 15	....	8J15	8J15	8J15	9 20	8 0	.....
GLASGOW (St. Enoch) .. ,,	....	9 25	..	11 0	1 30	..	2 30	..	5 30	..	9 30	9 30	9 30	11 0	9 15	..
AYR ,,	..	9 5	....	10 45	1 5	....	2 10	....	5 30	....	9 30	9 30	9 30	..	9 15	.....
CARLISLE .. .. ,,	11 50	12 0	1 12	1 30	3 55	4 45	5 8	5 50	8 15	8 45	12 25	12 45	1 5	1 50	12K 7	12K25
MANCHESTER (Victoria) .. arr.	3 25	3 25	4 40	4 40	..	8 15	8 15	9 25	12 10	12 10	..	..	4 35	..	4 35	4 35
LIVERPOOL (Exchange) .. ,,	3 25	3 25	4 45	4 45	....	8 18	8 18	9 15	12 10	12 10	....	....	4 45	...	4 45	4 45
BRADFORD ,,	3H 0	3H 0	4F20	4F20	6B55	7 40	..	9C 5	11 18	11 40	..	3 20	....	....	2 55	2 55
LEEDS .. .. ,,	2 8	2 20	3 40	3 56	6 15	7 7	....	9 0	11 10	11 30	2 52	3 10	..	4 10	2 35	2 52
SHEFFIELD ,,	3 15	3 32	5 20	5 20	7 6	8 8	..	11 19	1 2	1 2	.	4 8	..	5 10	3 57	3 57
DERBY .. .. ,,	4 28	4 28	6 0	6 0	8 17	9 47	....	12 28	1 50	1 50	....	5 35	....	7 3	5 35	5 35
BIRMINGHAM ,,	5 32	5 32	7 12	7 12	9 30	11 30	..	2 7	3 10	3 10	..	7E 5	..	9 5	7 5	7 5
CARDIFF .. .. ,	9 30	9 30	10 35	10 35	2 21	....	....	....	7L 9	7L 9	....	11E27	....	2 5	1 20	1 20
BRISTOL ,,	7 50	7 50	9 35	9 35	12 0	.	..	5 40	6 0	6 0	..	10E 0	..	12 40	10 48	10 48
PLYMOUTH .. .. ,,	12 5	12 5	4A34	....	4A34	....	....	....	10E55	10E55	....	2L12	....	3 45	3N30	3N30
NOTTINGHAM ,,	4 13	4 13	5 24	5 56	8 7	9 10	..	1 37	2 40	2 40	..	5 17	..	6 0	5 1	5 1
LEICESTER .. .. ,,	4 5	4 48	6 2	6 2	9 13	9 13	....	1 39	2 40	2 40	5 4	6E57	....	6 57	4 50	6 57
LONDON (ST PANCRAS) ,,	6 5	6 15	7 50	8 0	10 30	11 10	..	4 20	4 45	4 45	7 10	7 50	..	8 5	7 0	7 35

Sundays, Carlisle to London: Arrivals on Mondays.

A—Plymouth (North Road). B—Via Leeds. C—9.15 p.m. on Saturdays. D—Monday mornings excepted. E—Arrives later on Sundays. F—Six minutes later on Saturdays. G—Plymouth (North Road). No connection on Saturdays. H—Via Leeds. On Saturdays passengers arrive at 3.42 p.m. I—This time will apply during July and August only. J—8.10 p.m. on Saturdays. K—Passengers for L. & Y. line leave Carlisle at 1.5 a m. L—Sundays excepted. M—Saturday nights excepted. N—Plymouth (North Road.) Until July 18th arrives at 3.45 p.m. P—5.50 p.m. on Saturdays. No connection on Sundays.

FOR COMPLETE TIME TABLE OF SCOTCH CONNECTIONS, SEE PAGES 126 to 129.

For Through Carriage Arrangements see pages 1 & 2.

MAIN LINE.—HELLIFIELD TO APPLEBY AND CARLISLE.

	WEEKDAYS.																						Sunday nights and Monday mornings.				
London (St. Pancras) ..dep.	..	12L 5	..	..	5 15	5 15	5 15	9 30	9 30	9 35	11 30	11 35	11 35	11 35	1 30	1 30	3 0	*7 30*	*8 30*	9 30	9 30	12 0	8 30	9 30	9 30	12 0	..
Bedford „	....	1E25	....	....	6 15	6 15	6 15	9 35	9 35	9 35	11 33	11 33	11 33	11 33	1 35	1 35	3 36	*7 45*	*7 50*	10 30	10 30	....	7 27	10 30	10 30	.. ..	....
Leicester „	..	2L30	..	..	7 20	7 20	7 20	11 28	11 28	11 28	1 31	1 31	1 31	1 31	3 27	3 27	4 35	*8 54*	*10 30*	10 35	10 35	2 0	10 30	8 10	8 10	2 0	..
Nottingham „	....	2 0	....	....	7 35	7 35	7 35	11 5	11 5	12 0	1 0	2 2	2 2	2 2	2 51	2 51	5 37	*9 19*	*9 19*	12 0	12 0	2 0	....	12 0	12 0	2 0	....
Bristol (Temple Mead)..dep.	..	8R15	..	..	*1*E *3*	*1*E *3*	*1*E *3*	..	..	..	9 45	9 45	9 45	9 45	12 20	12 20	2 10	*6 5*	*6 5*	7 55	7 55	8 15	..	7 55	7 55	..	..
Bournemouth „	....	4R25	....	....	6R45	6R45	6R45	....	....	....	....	....	....	....	9 40	9 40	11 30	*1 50*	*1 50*	4 25	4 25	4 25	....	....	....	....	....
Bath „	..	7R35	..	..	11R 0	11R 0	11R 0	..	..	..	8 42	8 42	8 42	8 42	11 55	11 55	1 55	*5 25*	*5 25*	7 35	7 35	7 35	..	6 40	6 40	..	..
Gloucester „	....	9R20	....	....	*2*E*15*	*2*E*15*	*2*E*15*	7 5	7 5	7 5	10 32	10 32	10 32	10 32	12 50	12 50	3 7	*7 0*	*7 0*	8 56	8 56	9 20	....	8 46	8 46	....	..
Southampton (Docks) „	..	5R20	..	..	..	..	..	..	..	..	..	..	..	..	7 30	7 30	10 25	*2 30*	*2 30*	5 20	5 20	5 20	..	..	..	..	..
Cheltenham „	....	9R34	....	....	*2*E*30*	*2*E*30*	*2*E*30*	7 22	7 22	7 22	10 45	10 45	10 45	10 45	1 19	1 19	3 20	*7 14*	*7 14*	9 13	9 13	9 34	....	9 4	9 4	....	....
Birmingham (New St.) „	..	11R25	..	..	*4*E *8*	*4*E *8*	*4*E *8*	10 12	10 12	10 12	11 50	11 50	11 50	11 50	2 25	2 25	4 28	*8 20*	*8 20*	10 33	10 33	11 25	..	10 33	10 33	11 25	..
Derby „	....	3E15	....	....	7 2	7 2	7 2	11 30	11 30	11 30	12 57	12 57	12 57	12 57	3 32	3 32	5 35	*9 5*	*9 5*	11 37	11 37	12 55	....	11 37	11 37	12 55	....
Buxton (via Hope) „	..	..	..	..	..	..	..	9 15	9 15	11 10	11 30	11 30	11 30	11 30	2 35	2 35	4 35	*7 32*	*7 32*	7 32	7 32	..	..	7 10	7 10	..	..
Sheffield „	....	4E16	....	....	9 0	9 0	9 0	12 13	12 13	1 3	2 5	2 12	2 12	2 12	4 2	4 2	6 46	*9 32*	*11 49*	12 35	12 35	1 58	11 49	12 35	12 35	1 58	..
					HC	HC		HC	HC	HC	HC	HC			HC			HC	HC	HC	HC	HC	HC	HC	HC	HC	....
Harrogate dep.	..	..	..	7 0	8 35	8 35	9 8	12 34	12 34	..	2 5	2 5	2 5	2 5	4 24	4 52	6 42	*10 27*	..	10 25	10 25	..	..	8 30	..	..	..
Leeds „	....	6H40	....	8 10	10 0	10 0	10 12	1 28	1 28	....	3 28	3 28	3 28	3 30	5 33	5 36	7 45	*11 23*	*12 42*	1 50	2 0	4 5	12 42	1 50	2 0	4 5	....
Bradford „	..	6H40	..	8 35	9 42	9 42	10 15	12K50	12K50	1 20	2 40	2 40	2 40	3 35	5 5	5 27	8 20	*10*K *0*	*10*K*50*	1 20	1 20	2K 5	10K25	1 20	1 20	2K 5	..
Keighley „	....	7H 9	*Mondays excepted.*	9 7	10 13	10 13	10 45	*12*P*55*	*12*P*55*	1 54	3 20	3 20	3 20	4 12	5 23	6 12	8 40	*Saturday nights and Sunday mornings excepted.*	*Saturday nights and Sunday mornings excepted.*	1 40	1 40	4 30	....	1 40	1 40	4 30	....
Ilkley „	..	*6*I *0*		8 10	10 4	10 4	10 4	..	..	12 50	2 12	2 12	2 12	2 12	..	5 25	8 20			..	..	..	..	..	..	..	..
Skipton dep.	....	7 4		9 34	10 38	10 43	11 5	*1*P*16*	*1*P*16*	2 24	3 35	3 35	3 35	4 40	5 40	6 30	*9 30*			1 56	1 56	..	..	1 56	1 56	..	..
Hellifield arr.	..	7 33		9 53	10 53	11 5	11 28	2 14	2 14	....	4 14	4 26	4 26	5 1	6 18	6 44	*9 50*			2 35	2 48	Sleeping Car—London to Glasgow. Breakfast Car—Carlisle to Glasgow (Sundays excepted).	....	2 35	2 48	....	....
Manchester (Vic.) dep.	....	5 30		6 13	9 35	9 35	9 35	12 30	12 30	...	2V25	2V25	2V25	2V25	4 40	4 40	6 30			12 50	12 50		....	12 50	12 50	....	....
Bolton (Trinity Street) „	..	5 48		7 0	9 54	9 54	9 54	12 48	12 48	..	2 43	2 43	2 43	2 43	4 58	4 58	6 55			1 10	1 10		..	1 10	1 10	..	..
Liverpool (Exc.) dep.	..	.		6 5	9 30	9 30	9 30	12 35	12 35	..	2 20	2 20	2 20	2 20	4 35	4 35	6 50			12 45	12 45		..	12 45	12 45	..	..
Blackburn dep.	....	6 32		8 7	10 25	10 25	10 25	1 27	1 27	....	3 22	3 22	3 22	3 22	5 34	5 40	8 27			1 48	1 48		....	1 48	1 48	....	..
Clitheroe „	..	6 59		8 34	10 15	10 15	10 15	1 43	1 43	..	3 41	3 41	3 41	3 54	5 50	6 8	8 53			..	..		..	..	..	..	..
Hellifield arr.	....	7 34		9 5	10 57	10 57	10 57	2 0	2 0	....	4 0	4 0	4 0	4 23	6 7	6 40	9 22			2 20	2 20		....	2 20	2 20	....	....
HELLIFIELD dep.	..	7 50	*8 20*	10 0	11 0	11 10	11 32	2 17	2 22	..	4 22	4 32	4 38	5 5	6 23	6 52	*9 52*			2 43	2 58		..	2 43	2 58	..	..
Long Preston	....	7 54	*8 24*	10 3	....	....	11 36	....	....	Luncheon Cars—London to Glasgow.	Dining Cars—London to Glasgow.	Dining Cars—London to Edinburgh.	....	5 9	Dining Cars—London to Glasgow.	6 55	*9 55*			....	....			....	....	..	..
Settle	..	8 2	*8 35*	10 10	..	..	11 45	Luncheon Cars—London to Edinburgh.	2 32				4 47	5 17		7 2	*10 2*									..	..
Horton	....	8 12		10 20	....	....	11 58		....				....	5 29		7B12	*10 15*									..	..
Ribblehead	..	8 21	..	10 29	..	..	12 10		2 48				..	5 39		..	....			Sleeping Car—London to Edinburgh.	Sleeping Car—London to Glasgow.		Sleeping Car—London to Dumfries.	Sleeping Car—London to Edinburgh	Sleeping Car—London to Glasgow.	Sleeping Car—London to Glasgow. Breakfast Car—Carlisle to Glasgow.	..
Dent	....	8 32	....	....	....	....	12 22		....				....	5 51		....											..
Hawes Junc. & Garsdale (for Hawes)	..	8 38	..	10 44	..	..	12G42		3C25				5 17	5 58		..											..
Kirkby Stephen & Ravenstonedale	....	8 53	....	10 59	....	....	12 58		3 43				5 32	6 14		....		Sleeping Car—London to Edinburgh, Perth, and Inverness.	..								..
Crosby Garrett	..	8 59	..	..	..	..	1 4		..				..	6 20		..	*Saturdays only—Skipton to Horton.*		Sleeping Car—London to Dumfries.								..
Ormside	....	9 8	....	....	....	....	1 13		....				....	6 29		....											..
Appleby	7 45	9 14	..	11 13	..	12 10	1 18		4 5				5 48	6 35		..											..
Via Appleby: Appleby (N.E.) dep.	....	....	....	12 24	....	12 24	2 59		4 34				....	7 22		....											..
Penrith (for Ullswater) arr.	..	..	..	12 58	..	12 58	3 34		4 55				..	8 5		..											..
Keswick „	....	....	....	1 50	....	1 50	5 55		5 55	....	....	....	....	9 10		....											..
Cockermouth „	..	..	..	2 23	..	2 23	6 30		6 30		..	..	..	9 40		..											..
Long Marton	7 51	9 21	....	11 19	....	....	1 26		4 16	....	....	....	T	6 41		....											..
New Biggin	7 57	9 27	..	11 25	..	..	1 32		4 22	..	..	..	5 59	6 47		..					....				..		..
Culgaith	8 1	9 31	....	....	....	....	1 36		4 27	....	....	....	T	6 51		....					..						..
Langwathby	8 8	9 38	..	11 32	..	..	1 42		4 35	..	..	..	6 8	6 58		..					....						..
Little Salkeld	8 12	9 42	....	11 36	....	....	1 48	....	4 40	....	....	....	6 12	7 2		....	....				..						..
Lazonby & Kirkoswald	8 18	9 48	..	11 42	..	Z	1 54	..	4 47	..	..	..	6 18	7 8		..	..				....		..		..		..
Armathwaite	8 28	9 58	....	11 51	Z	....	2 6	....	4 57	....	....	....	6 28	7 18		....	....				..	..	....		....		..
Cotehill	8 34	10 4	..	..	..	..	2 12	..	5 3	..	..	..	6 34	7 24		..	..				....	..	..		..		..
Cumwhinton	8 40	10 10	....	12 1	....	....	2 18	....	5 9	....	....	....	6 40	7 30	....	....	....		....		..	....	....		....		..
Scotby	8 45	10 14	..	..			2 22	..	5 14	..			6 44	7 34		..	..		..	..	..	..	..	..	..	..	..
CARLISLE arr.	8 50	10 20	....	12 10	12 35	12 45	2 30	3 45	5 20	4 5	5 50	6 0	6 50	7 40	7 55	....	....	*1 30*	*2 55*	4 15	4 30	6 25	2 55	4 15	4 30	6 25	....
																				Arrivals on Weekdays. / Arrivals on Sundays.	Arrivals on Weekdays. / Arrivals on Sundays.	Arrivals on Weekdays. / Arrivals on Sundays.					Arrivals on Mondays.
Dumfries arr.	10 39	11 55	..	..	1 27	..	4 38	4 49	6 35	4 49	6 35	..	..	O	O	..	..	..	*3 50*	5 14 / 5 38	5 14 / 5 38	7 9 / 7 9	3 50	5 14	5 14	7 9	
Kilmarnock „	2 15	2 15	....	..	2 44	....	6 0	6 0	7 48	6 0	7 48	....	....	9 46	9 46	....	....	....	*5 26*	6 29 / 7 2	6 29 / 7 2	8 24 / 8 24	5 26	6 29	6 29	8 24	
Greenock „	4 37	4 37	..	..	4 37	..	8 2	8 2	9 52	8 2	9 52	..	..	12 5	12 5	..	..	..	*7 26*	8 42 / 8 48	8 42 / 8 48	10 20 / 10 15	7 26	8 42	8 42	10 20	
Glasgow (St. Enoch) „	3 5	3 5	....	....	3 20	....	6 35	6 35	8 25	6 35	8 25	....	....	10 20	10 20	....	....	....	*6 10*	7 5 / 7 45	7 5 / 7 45	9 0 / 9 0	6 10	7 5	7 5	9 0	
Hawick „	10 15	..	..	..	..	2 5	5 14	..	7 13	..	..	7 13	..	9 5	9 5	..	..	..	..	5 28 / 5 28	.. / ..	10 1 / ..	..	5 28	..	10 1	
Melrose „	11 4	....	....	....	....	2 31	6 0	....	7 38	....	....	7 38	....	M	M	....	....	....	....	6 36 / 8 28	.... /	11 4 /	....	6 30	....	11 4	
Edinburgh (Waverley) „	12 5	..	..	..	..	3 30	6 5	6 5	8 35	..	..	8 35	..	10 25	10 25	..	..	*3 50*	..	6 45 / 6 45	.. / ..	12 5 / ..	..	6 45	..	12 5	
Dundee „	3 37	....	....	....	....	6 15	8 10	8 10	10 51	....	....	10 51	....	....	....	....	....	*5 28*	....	9 5 / 9 15	.... /	3 37 /	....	9 5	....	3 37	
Aberdeen „	6 0	..	..	..	..	8 40	10 5	10 5	12 50	..	..	12 50	..	..	..	..	..	*7 20*	..	11 10 / 11 20	.. / ..	6 0 / ..	..	11 10	..	6 0	
Perth „	3 5	....	....	....	....	6 20	7 52	7 52	10 36	....	....	10 36	....	....	....	....	....	*5 5*	....	8 55 / 8 40	.... /	3 5 /	....	8 55	....	3 5	
Inverness „	8 35	..	..	..	..	..	12 10	12 10	5J10	..	..	5J10	..	..	..	..	..	*9 10*	..	1 50 / 1 30	.. / ..	8 35 / ..	..	1 50	..	8 35	

B—Runs forward Settle to Horton on Fridays only when required.

C—Arrives Hawes Junction at 3.5 p.m.

E—Monday mornings excepted.

G—Arrives Hawes Junction at 12.32 p.m.

H—Leeds 6.0, Bradford 6.10, and Keighley 6.43 a.m., after September 12th.

I—Tuesdays and Saturdays only.

J—No connection to Inverness on Sundays.

K—Passengers from Bradford to Carlisle and Scotland travel via Leeds.

L—Passengers leave St. Pancras at 12.0 midnight on Sundays and Leicester 2.0 on Monday mornings.

M—Sets down passengers from Midland Line when required.

O—Sets down passengers from the Midland System.

P—Keighley 12.46 and Skipton 1.4 p.m. on Saturdays.

R—Saturday nights excepted.

T—Sets down passengers from Appleby and South thereof when required.

V—Calls at Salford on Tuesdays when required to take up passengers for Stations North of Hellifield.

Z—Sets down passengers from Clitheroe and beyond, also from Keighley and South thereof, when required.

HC — **HORSES & PRIVATE CARRIAGES** are not conveyed by these Trains except as notified below, or by special arrangement under exceptional circumstances:—

10.0 a.m. from Leeds. To Carlisle and Scotland.

7.30 p.m. from London for Edinburgh and beyond.

7.55 p.m. from Bristol. For Carlisle and Scotland.

8.30 and 9.30 p.m. and 12.0 midnight rom London. From London to Carlisle and Scotland.

For Through Carriage arrangements see pages 1 and 2.

Trains shewn in italics run only as indicated.

MAIN LINE.—CARLISLE and APPLEBY to HELLIFIELD.

A thin line between the hour and minute figures indicates p.m.

WEEKDAYS.

Station		Mondays only. Carlisle to Hellifield.	Mondays excepted. Settle to Hellifield.		Goes forward from Hawes Junction at 1.15 p.m.	Luncheon Cars—Carlisle to London.	Luncheon Cars—Glasgow to London.		Dining Cars—Edinburgh to London.	Dining Cars—Glasgow to London.	Saturdays excepted. Goes forward from Appleby at 3.55 p.m.	Saturdays only. Goes forward from Appleby at 3.55 p.m.		Dining Cars—Glasgow to London.			Dining Cars—Edinburgh to London.				Tea Car Glasgow to Carlisle.		Saturdays only.	Sleeping Car—Glasgow to London. Times of arrival, Tuesday to Sunday mornings inclusive.	Sleeping Car—Edinburgh to London. Times of arrival Tuesday to Sunday mornings inclusive.	Arrivals on Mondays.	Sleeping Cars—Inverness, Perth, Edinburgh Saturday nights and Sunday mornings excepted and Glasgow to London. Times of arrival Tuesday to Saturday mornings inclusive.	Sunday nights & Monday mornings. Sleeping Car—Glasgow to London. Arrivals on Mondays.	Sunday nights & Monday mornings. Sleeping Car—Edinburgh to London. Arrivals on Mondays.	Sunday nights & Monday mornings. Arrivals on Mondays.
Inverness .. dep.						10A30	10A30		10A30								8 40	8 40	8 40			11 10			3 50	3 50	*5 30*		10 10	
Perth ,,						6 30	6 30		8 35								12 30	12 30	12 30			4 10			7 55	7 55	*9 40*		4 10	
Aberdeen ,,									6 20								10 20	10 20	10 20			1 25			5 30	5 30	*7 45*		8 30	
Dundee ,,						6 40	6 40		8 10								12 20	12 20	12 20			3 35			7 30	7 30	*9 35*		5 30	
Edinburgh (Waverley) ,,						9 30	9 30		10 30								2 15	2 15	2 35			6 0			10 0	10 15	*11 30*		9 30	
Melrose ,,						8 9	8 9		11 32								2 35	2 35	3 37			7 2			11 2	11 9			10 33	
Hawick ,,				6 0		8 52	8 52		12 1					12 10	12 10		3B32	3B32	4 11			7 29			11 29	11 50			10 59	
Glasgow (St. Enoch) ,,							9 25			11 0				1 30	1 30			2 30	2 30	3 0	5 30			9 30	9 30	9 30	*11 0*	9 15	9 15	
Greenock ,,							8 25			10 0				12 30	12 30			1 10	1 10	1 10	4 15			8M15	8M15	8M15	*9W20*	8 0	8 0	
Kilmarnock ,,							9 59		10 5	11 38				2 4	2 4			3 6	3 6	3 40	6 7			10 10	10 10	10 10	*11 35*	9 55	9 55	
Dumfries ,,							11 14		11 50	12 45				D	2 50			4 20	4 20	5 25	7 20			11 31	11 31	11 31	*12 50*	11 18	11 18	
					HC	HC	HC		HC	HC				HC			HC	HC	HC		HC	HC		HC	HC	HC	HC	HC	HC	HC
CARLISLE dep.		*6 30*		8 35	10 55	11 50	12 0		1 12	1 30	*1 55*	*2 25*		3 55	4 0		4 45	5 8	5 50	6 45	8 15	8 45		12 25	12 45	1 5	*1 50*	12 7	12 25	1 5
Scotby				8 41	11 1						*2 1*	*2 33*			4 6					6 52										
Cumwhinton		*6 39*		8 46	11 5						*2 6*	*2 39*			4 11					6 56										
Cotehill		*6 46*		8 53	11 12						*2 13*	*2 46*			4 18					7 3										
Armathwaite		*6 52*		8 59	11 18						*2 20*	*2 55*			4 25				6 6	7 10	8 31									
Lazonby & Kirkoswald		*7 2*		9 9	11 27						*2 30*	*3 7*			4 36				6 16	7 21										
Little Salkeld		*7 8*		9 15	11 33						*2 36*	*3 14*			4 43					7 27										
Langwathby		*7 13*		9 20	11 37						*2 41*	*3 20*			4 49				6 25	7 33	8 47									
Culgaith		*7 19*		9 26	11 43						*2 47*	*3 27*			4 56					7 39										
New Biggin		*7 23*		9 30	11 47						*2 52*	*3 32*			5 0					7 43										
Long Marton		*7 29*		9 36	11 53						*2 59*	*3 39*			5 6					7 49										
Via Appleby: Cockermouth dep.					8 20								1 15		1 15		1 15	1 15			6 4									
Via Appleby: Keswick ,,					9 0								1 50		1 50		1 50	1 50			6 35									
Via Appleby: Penrith (for Ullswater) ,,				7 20	10 35								2 52		4 10		4 10	4 10			7 28									
Via Appleby: Appleby (N.E.) arr.				7 58	11 7								3 13		4 59		4 59	4 59			7 58									
Appleby		*7 35*		9 46	12 2						*3 5*	*3 45*	3 55		5J25		C	5 47	6 40	7 55	9 2	E								
Ormside		*7 42*		9 52	12 8								4 2		5 36															
Crosby Garrett		*7 53*		10 3	12 19								4 13		5 47															
Kirkby Stephen & Ravenstonedale		*8 0*		10 10	12 27								4 20		5 54				I											
Hawes Junc. & Garsdale (for Hawes)		*8 17*		10 30	12 41		1 10	1 16					4 36		6K10			6 22	I		9 38	I								
Dent		*8 23*		10 37	☛								4 43		6 37															
Ribblehead		*8 34*		10 48				L					4 54		6 48															
Horton	7 5	*8 42*		10 55				1 34					5 0		6 55								*10 30*							
Settle	7 15	*8 53*	*9 0*	11 6				1 43					5 10		7 5	5 57			7 37		10 1	E	*10 43*							
Long Preston	7 22	*8 59*	*9 9*	11 14				1 49					5 17		7 12	6 7							*10 53*							
HELLIFIELD arr.	7 25	*9 2*	*9 12*	11 17				1 52	2 47	3 5			5 20		7 15	6 11	6 20	6 49	7 45		10 10	10 28	*10 56*			2 40				2 40
Hellifield dep.	7 35	10 0	10 0	11 57				1 56	3 20	3 20			6 5		7 50	6 53		6 52	7 50		10 40	10 40				3 0				3 0
Clitheroe arr.	8 10	10 30	10 30	12 27			2 48	2 48	I	I			6 41		8 7	7 47		7 47	8 7		Q	Q								
Blackburn ,,	8 39	11 1	11 1	12 58			2 27	2 27	3 52	3 52			7 12		8 25	7 23		7 23	8 25		11 15	11 15				3 34				3 34
Liverpool (Exch.) arr.	10 16	12 30	12 30	3 5			3 25	3 25	4 45	4 45			8 18		9 15	8 18		8 18	9 15		12 10	12 10				4 45				4 45
Bolton (Trinity Street) arr.	9 29	11 40	11 40	1 46			3 5	3 5	4 20	4 20			7 54		9 3	7 54		7 54	9 3		11 50	11 50				4 15				4 15
Manchester (Salf'd) ,,	9 55	11 55	11 55	2 5			3 20	3 20	4 35	4 35			8 9		9 19	8 9		8 9	9 19		12 5	12 5								
Manchester (Vic.) ,,	10 0	12 0	12 0	2 10			3 25	3 25	4 40	4 40			8 15		9 25	8 15		8 15	9 25		12 10	12 10				4 35				4 35
Hellifield dep.	7 35	9 21	9 21	11 24				2 18	2 55	3 13			5 43		7 55	6 24	6 24		7 55		10 18	10 38								
Skipton arr.	7 55	9 37	9 37	11 38				2 36	3 39	3 39			6 2		8 12	6 49	6 49		8 12		10 31	I			2 35				2 14	
Ilkley arr.	9 3	10 40	10 40	2 1				4 11	4 11	4 11			*8J 0*		9 30	*8U 0*	*8U 0*		9 30											
Keighley ,,	8 20	9 57	9 57	11 56				2 54	3C55	3C55			6 25		8 30	7 8	7 8		8 30		10 47	I			2 58				2 35	
Bradford ,,	8 42	10 20	10 20	12 35		3R 0	3R 0	3 22	4C20	4C20			6 53	6N55	9V 5	7 40	7 40		9V 5		11 18	11H40			3 20				2 55	
Leeds ,,	9 5	10 50	10 50	12 20		2 8	2 20	3 34	3 40	3 56			6 56	6 15	9 0	7 7	7 7		9 0		11 10	11 30		2 52	3 10		*4 10*	2 35	2 52	
Harrogate ,,	10 20	11 44	11 44	1 16		3 19	3 19	5 4	5 4	5 4			8 10	7 20	10 0	8 10	8 10		10 0					5S51	5S51		*5 51*	5 51	5 51	
Sheffield arr.	10 52	12 0	12 0	1 29		3 15	3 32	5 20	5 20	5 20			8 8	7 6	11 19	8 8	8 8		11 19		1 2	1 2			4 8		*5 10*	3 57	3 57	
Buxton (via Hope) ,,	12 15	1 40	1 40	4 42		5 42	5 42	7 22	7 22	7 22			9 42	9 42		9 42	9 42								9 58		*9 58*	9 25	9 25	
Derby ,,	12 25	12 40	12 40	2 30		4 28	4 28	6 0	6 0	6 0			9 47	8 17	12 28	9 47	9 47		12 28		1 50	1 50			5 35		*7 3*	5 35	5 35	
Birmingham (New St.) ,,	1 25	1 40	1 40	3 30		5 32	5 32	7 12	7 12	7 12			11 30	9 30	2 7	11 30	11 30		2 7		3 10	3 10			7S 5		*9 5*	7 5	7 5	
Cheltenham ,,	2 45	2 45	2 45	4 33		6 37	6 37	8 17	8 17	8 17				10 43	4 15				4 15		4 28	4 28			8S44		*11 31*	9 36	9 36	
Southampton (Docks) ,,	6 0	6 0	6 0			9 50	9 50								8 18				8 18		8 18	8 18			1T47		*5 33*	1 47	1 47	
Gloucester ,,	2 42	2 59	2 59	4 54		6 51	6 51	8 32	8 32	8 32				10 57	4 35				4 35		4 47	4 47			8S58		*11 45*	9 50	9 50	
Bath ,,	4 2	4 2	4 2	5 58		8 20	8 20	10 8	10 3	10 3					6 47				6 47		6 47	6 47			10F15		*2 15*	12 7	12 7	
Bournemouth ,,	6 10	6 10	6 10	8 15											11 0				11 0		11 0	11 0			1T 0		*4 15*	3 16	8 16	
Bristol (Temple Mead) ,,	3 35	8 55	3 55	5 35		7 50	7 50	9 35	9 35	9 35				12 0	5 40				5 40		6 0	6 0			10F 0		*12 40*	10 48	10 48	
Nottingham arr.	1 6	1 6	1 6	2 32		4 13	4 13	5 24	5 24	5 56			9 10	8 7	1 37	9 10	9 10		1 37		2 40	2 40			5 17		*6 0*	5 1	5 1	
Leicester ,,	12 13	2 5	2 5	3 37		4 5	4 48	6 2	6 2	6 2			9 13	9 13	1 39	9 13	9 13		1 39		2 40	2 40		5 4	6S57		*6 57*	4 50	6 57	
Bedford ,,	1 57	2 39	2 39	4 40		4 54	5 54	7 28	7 28	7 28					3 6				3 6		4 10	4 10			6T50		*8 39*	6 33	6 33	
London (St. Pancras) ,,	2 10	3 40	3 40	5 0		6 5	6 15	7 50	7 50	8 0			11 10	10 30	4 20	11 10	11 10		4 20		4 45	4 45		7 10	7 50		*8 5*	7 0	7 35	

A—Saturday and Sunday nights excepted from Inverness.

B—Takes up passengers for Midland Line when required.

C—Takes up passengers for Leeds and stations South thereof.

D—Takes up passengers for Leeds and Stations South thereof.

E—Sets down passengers from the North British line.

F—Passengers leaving Scotland on Saturday nights arrive at these stations on Sunday nights.

G—Six minutes later on Saturdays.

H—This arrival time refers to passengers from Carlisle and Scotland only.

I—Sets down from Carlisle and Scotland.

J—Arrives Appleby at 5.15 p.m.

K—Leaves Hawes Junction at 6.28 p.m.

L—Takes up passengers for L. & Y. Line.

M—8.10 p.m. on Saturdays.

N—Passengers from Carlisle and Scotland for Bradford travel via Leeds.

O—Sets down from North of Hellifield.

Q—Calls at Whalley on Saturdays only to set down from stations beyond Hellifield.

R—Passengers from Carlisle and Scotland for Bradford travel *via* Leeds, and on Saturdays arrive at 3.42 p.m.

S—Arrives later on Sundays.

T—Sundays excepted.

U—Saturdays excepted.

V—9.15 p.m. on Saturdays.

W—This time will apply during July and August only.

LP—Stops when required to take up London passengers.

HC—HORSES AND PRIVATE CARRIAGES are not conveyed by these Trains except as notified below, or by special arrangement under exceptional circumstances:—

10.55 a.m., 1.12, 1.30, 5.50, 8.15, and 8.45 p.m. and 1.5 a.m. from Carlisle. From Carlisle and Scotland to stations beyond Hellifield.

12.45 a.m. (12.25 a.m. Mondays) from Carlisle. From Carlisle and Scotland to stations beyond Sheffield.

1.50 a.m. from Carlisle. From Scotland to London.

For Through Carriage arrangements see pages 1 & 2.

Trains shewn in Italics run only as indicated.

Along the route

Above:
An excellent picture of the start of the S&C just beyond the divergence of the Lancaster and Carnforth line at Settle Junction. 'Britannia' 4-6-2 No 70054 *Dornoch Firth* is making a speedy approach with the afternoon Glasgow-Leeds express in June 1961. *Derek Cross*

Above:
A telling illustration of the Long Drag, near Helwith Bridge on the 1 in 100 climb. 'Duchess' 4-6-2 No 46229 *Duchess of Hamilton* heads the northbound 'Cumbrian Mountain Express' of 4 February 1984. *W. A. Sharman*

Left:
A less familiar view of Batty Moss Viaduct, Ribblehead with a '9F' 2-10-0 southbound with a ballast train in October 1966. *G. P. Cooper*

Below left:
Beyond Batty Moss it is clear that the railway has no alternative but to tunnel under Blea Moor. A 'Jubilee' 4-6-0 in its last days of service is approaching Blea Moor signalbox with a northbound freight. *R. Hewitt*

Left:
The S&C style of station. This is Dent, in May 1967. *J. Scrace*

Below:
The subsidiary cross valleys leading into Dentdale could only be traversed by expensive, lofty viaducts. The route taken by the railway along the hillside may be picked out in this 20 August 1966 view of LMS '5' 4-6-0 No 44911 crossing Arten Gill Viaduct with a southbound freight. Derelict snow fences are in the foreground. *Maurice S. Burns*

Right:
This photograph shows the carefully chosen route up to the summit at Ais Gill. A pair of Class 25s are heading down grade, away from Ais Gill to Shotlock Hill Tunnel, with an up cement train on 23 July 1976. *C. R. Davis*

Below:
Armathwaite was one of the most attractive of the line's stations, and fortunately is still used by Dalesrail workings, although much of its character has gone. Already under sentence of death, one of the stopping trains, the 08.35 Carlisle–Skipton, calls at the station on 10 May 1969. *Geoffrey J. Jackson*

Bottom:
If the moorland scenery is grand, the quiet, pastoral environment of the Eden Valley has a special magic. LMS '5' 4-6-0 No 44706 and 'Royal Scot' 4-6-0 No 46109 *Royal Engineer* are well into their stride between Langwathby and Culgaith with a heavy up 'Thames-Clyde Express' of 7 July 1956. *R. Leslie*

Snows of 1947

F. Slindon

I was involved in operations over the Settle & Carlisle line in that memorable winter and have been asked on several occasions to write about my experiences. In doing so, the reader must appreciate that so much time has elapsed that it is quite impossible to be completely accurate. In the history of this section of railway, snowstorms have blocked the lines on several occasions for periods of up to two weeks, as indeed they did in 1947. What made that winter special was that the storm returned and the blockage was extended to eight weeks. Before describing the incidents of February/March 1947, I ought to outline the special features of the section between Settle Junction and Kirkby Stephen known as the Long Drag, which runs along the foothills of a range of mountains and through deep cuttings. In the down direction, the gradient rises for the first 14 miles at the rate of 1 in 100 to a point about half a mile inside Blea Moor Tunnel. The line then undulates to Ais Gill signalbox which stands at 1,169ft above sea level. In the up direction, from Carlisle the railway commences by climbing moderately to Appleby. From there, it rises more steeply to Kirkby Stephen, where the Long Drag starts and the gradient rises at 1 in 100.

Blockages by snow on the Settle & Carlisle are caused by freak winds known as the Helm Winds which may last for three days. Even if there is only a moderate fall of snow on the ground, the winds pick up the snow and deposit it on the track, and in the case of 1947, cuttings were filled to the height of the overbridges. Nothing can be done under these circumstances to keep the line open for traffic and it is important to stop trains as quickly as possible from entering the area otherwise they would cause blockages which would impede and delay the clearance of the lines.

Precautions were taken to cope with emergencies created by snowstorms. A number of '4F' 0-6-0s were adapted for the fitting of steel snowploughs at the chimney end by Skipton and Hellifield motive power depots. In the autumn, several of these engines had the ploughs fitted ready for use and during winter months they were not allowed out of the district. Several goods brake vans were converted into mess vans with accommodation for six men and were equipped with the necessary tools as well as a portable telephone to help communicate with signalboxes when necessary. When in action each snowplough was in the charge of an operating inspector, a station master or relief signalman, a loco inspector and fitter, and a permanent way inspector. The ploughs ran back to back with the plough brake between, thereby allowing movement in either direction.

Being in the centre of the area, a small loco depot was set up at Dent. This included accommodation for 10 men with bunking and messing facilities and when necessary a loco inspector and fitter also attended. A

Right:
Dent station, from the south, fairly early in the 1947 snows. Dent's up home bracket signal to the centre, with Hellifield's steam crane buried in the snow.
W. Hubert Foster per John W. Holroyd

Above:
Mallerstang Common during the 1962/63 winter with Kingmoor LMS '5' 4-6-0 No 45466 on a snow clearing train. *Peter Brock*

Left:
Hellifield shed on 25 January 1953, showing two of the shed's snowplough '4Fs', No 44149 (centre) with a cover over the tender coal space for use with a large plough and No 44282 (right) which has a tender cab and is intended for use with a medium plough.

wagon of coal was placed in position in the late autumn to provide a stock of fuel. Plug points were installed in each platelayer's cabin and on walls at various locations so that the plough crews could contact the signalmen on their portable telephones. All equipment was tested in the autumn to make sure it was working properly.

On Sunday, 3 February 1947, a slight fall of snow had been reported in the area. Several snowploughs were fitted to engines which were steamed and made ready for manning. During the night snow fell again, accompanied by rising winds, so two sets of ploughs were turned out in the charge of relief signalmen. The night trains got through but the snowploughs experienced difficulty in keeping the lines clear. Shortly after I arrived on duty we were told that one of the ploughs had derailed at Blea Moor and the other one was coming into Hellifield for servicing and to raise steam.

It was agreed I should take charge of this plough when it was ready to leave Hellifield shed. Once under way we had little difficulty in reaching Horton where we were told that the down express which had been doing badly when passing that point had come to a stand about a mile from Ribblehead. I immediately contacted the operating manager at Leeds and advised him of the circumstances. We both realised the importance of moving the express as quickly as possible and he agreed that once the express was clear of the area the line should be closed to traffic and handed over to the snowploughs. The station master and early-turn signalman volunteered to accompany us and help to free the express. We set off towards Ribblehead over the up line and drew alongside the train and I advised its driver that we intended crossing over to the down line at Ribblehead. Then we would plough back towards the front of his train. He agreed to look out for us and guide us back to the express. Arriving at Ribblehead, we cleared the snow from the crossover road and crossed to the down line. Our next job was to find a set of catch-points about half a mile to the south. Having located them we cleared them of snow, clipped them up, and proceeded towards the train, stopping about

Scenes from the 1947 snows — 1. (*Above*) The first overbridge north of Dent. In the second blockage of that winter this bridge was completely covered. (*Above right*) Officers' inspection saloon on tour. (*Right*) Dent station looking toward Dent Head.
W. Hubert Foster per John W. Holroyd

Below:
Scenes from the 1947 snows — 2. Soldiers and PoWs loading snow in Shale Cutting and Dent Head on 19 March 1947.

50 yards short, at which point its driver was waiting for us. We cleared snow from under the locomotive and a short distance ahead, and threw some sand under the locomotive's wheels and on the rails ahead. The driver agreed that he should be able to move. I asked him to send his fireman back to Selside signalbox and to stay there until I had spoken to him from Ribblehead. Then he was to return to the train and tell the driver to proceed to Ribblehead. The ploughs moved forward to Blea Moor. I spoke to the driver again from there and we agreed that we should carry on in this manner moving from box to box. We did very well until approaching Mallerstang where the signals were against us and a freight train was standing on the up line. I went to the signalbox there and asked why we were being held up, to be told that at the south end of Birkett tunnel, about half a mile ahead, the line was blocked by snow; according to the local ganger snow completely filled the tunnel-mouth. The plough drivers, well experienced in this type of thing, reckoned that as the snow was freshly fallen, and the plough was on a falling gradient, we should be able to force our way through. All the time the weather continued to worsen. I spoke to the driver of the express which was now standing at Ais Gill and told him not to move the train until I contacted him from Kirkby Stephen. So we forced our way through Birkett tunnel and on arrival at Kirkby Stephen I informed the driver of the express of the conditions at the tunnel, warning him

Above left:
Dent, looking towards Dent Head.
F. Slindon, W. Hubert Foster per John W. Holroyd

Above:
The snows of later years. Dent station during the 1962/63 winter. *Peter Brock*

Left:
On 20 January 1963, an LMS '5' 4-6-0 takes a northbound freight through Dent station, when single line working was in operation.
Peter Brock

that he could expect a lot of snow to have fallen back on to the track due to the very confined space at the mouth of the tunnel. He should approach the tunnel at reduced speed to avoid any undue shock to the passengers, relying on the falling gradient and the weight of the train to get him through. We were very relieved to see the express approaching Kirkby Stephen. I spoke to the driver and told him that we would follow him to Appleby. When we arrived there, I was pleased to find that there were no injuries to any of the passengers and that the train was undamaged. The passengers had been kept well-supplied with refreshments including milk for the babies on board.

Now we faced the problem of getting back to our base at Hellifield, remembering that there was still the train standing at Mallerstang. There was surprisingly little snow at Appleby which proved that the Helm Winds are mainly responsible for the problem of drifting on the Long Drag. I contacted Control at Carlisle whose district we were now in, to be informed that arrangements had already been made to stop any trains entering the area; instead, they were being diverted via Settle Junction, Clapham and Low Gill. At about 7.30pm, we set off over the down line, running wrong road to Ais Gill and arrived at Hellifield about 9pm. The conditions throughout the area were now much worse, the Long Drag being completely unfit for trains to enter. From this stage, with every plough engaged and staff drafted in to assist from elsewhere in the area, I can only give the highlights of the operations in which I actually took part.

The passenger trains taking the diversionary route suffered on average about 40min delay, but freights were much worse off mainly, I suspect, due to being side-tracked on the West Coast route for other trains to pass. By the morning of Friday 14 February, the winds had calmed and so the ploughs made good progress in clearing the line.

The only section over which nothing had passed since being blocked was the up line between Mallerstang and Ais Gill. When we arrived at Ais Gill that Friday morning, it was to find that a light engine had derailed on the crossover road there, blocking the up line, and the Leeds steam crane was engaged in rerailing it. There was a set of ploughs at Mallerstang with a gang of workmen. The man in charge of them said that he had been to Ais Gill and back over the down line with a plough so as to inspect the up line; the conditions were very bad with deep drifts at each end and many smaller ones in-between. The crane was blocking the up line and so we travelled through to Mallerstang over the down line so that the plough crew and I could access the position. We decided that we had a chance of tackling the job from the Mallerstang end.

An old wooden framed goods brake van was marshalled between the ploughs and all agreed that it was too risky to take this with us; there was the danger of it collapsing when we hit the large and well-settled drift at the north end. So the brake was taken out and left at Kirkby Stephen. We explained our intentions to the signalmen at Mallerstang and Ais Gill. The former agreed to give us a clear run while the Ais Gill signalman reminded us of the situation in his section. We got both engines blowing off and at Mallerstang signalbox we were going at full speed. Here we were completely blotted out and with all of us prepared for the shock took no harm. We were slowing down quickly and our engine, which was leading, got its motion completely blocked up and started sliding, being propelled by the rear engine which was ramming us from behind. We came out of the drift at walking speed but very soon our engine got going again and continued at a steady pace, running into and out of the drifts. Then we sighted Ais Gill's up distant signal and our next problem was to hit the drift outside the home signal with enough momentum to clear the way. We had agreed a special code to do this which worked perfectly and so we were through. The light engine which had been a casualty at Ais Gill had now been rerailed so we went forward to Garsdale to clear the road for the crane to depart. On arrival at Garsdale the officers' coach from Leeds was there and we were congratulated on our efforts. But to say that the lines were 'clear' is rather misleading for only the space between the rails was free of snow. On each side of the tracks and in the space we know as the 'six-foot', snow was piled several feet high. Viewed from the signalbox the up and down lines looked like two canals.

I thought that we should continue to divert trains away from the Settle & Carlisle a little longer to avoid the lines becoming blocked again if the Helm Wind returned. However,

Regional headquarters insisted that if the tracks were clear the trains must run. Accordingly, arrangements were made for all freight train loads to be reduced by 50%, with the snowploughs remaining in action, running ahead in front of each train when considered necessary. Throughout the area, roads were blocked for many weeks and helicopters were used to drop cattle-food and bales of hay into farms. Where possible, all cattle were gathered up and put under cover and in the stock yards but many of them and almost all the sheep left out starved. During the second blockage, one farmer told me that he was completely out of food for his stock although he had three wagonloads of hay consigned to him. When I got back to Skipton that night, I found the three wagons and arranged that they would be moved by the light engines booked to depart at 5.30 the next morning. The farmer was waiting for us. We took off the ropes and sheets and pushed the bales down the embankment for him to take away by sledge. To underline the hazards to farm animals left out, at one stage there was a freak rain shower and any animals not under cover were frozen to death in a coat of ice. I saw rabbits and hares in the fields which had suffered this fate. Within a few days the Helm Winds returned, the air was full of snow and it was then difficult to tell how much of it was fresh and how much had been whipped up from the ground. Snowploughs were travelling ahead of all trains, often needing to travel back and make a second run. Snow and ice were becoming so hard-packed in the 'four-foot' that engines and vehicles were running off the rails. On Ribblehead viaduct this happened to the engine hauling the Hellifield steam crane which I was conducting with the purpose of rerailing a ballast van that had run off at Blea Moor. Block signalling was suspended between Helwith Bridge and Kirkby Stephen, the lines once more being handed over to the district engineer for clearance.

A meeting was held to decide how best to deal with the general situation. The first requirement was that the track from Dent Head should be cleared far enough on the down line to allow room for three sets of wagons to be placed for loading. Afterwards the snow was to be unloaded over Ribblehead viaduct, Arten Gill viaduct and down embankments at other suitable points. The following trains were scheduled:

1. An engineers' special train to depart Leeds at 06.00 conveying staff and refreshments.
2. A train of eight coaches to depart Otley conveying soldiers.
3. A train of eight coaches to depart Skipton conveying Italian and German prisoners of war.

Each of these trains was to arrive on site at Dent Head between 07.00 and 08.00.

The first job was to force our way in on the down road. The ploughs stuck continually and it took an hour or more in each case to dig them out again. We reached a point, in Shale Cutting, north of Dent Head, where the snow was at its deepest and, rather than waste time in pushing through to where it was easier, I decided to get a class '8' engine which was standing at Blea Moor to come through and be marshalled between the two snowploughs. We set back a good distance and hit the drift, managing to cut through at the first attempt. Now we were ready to commence the new programme. The assembled team was to clear the south side of Dent while Carlisle agreed to clear to the north. During this period my job was to accompany the three locomotives which left Skipton every day at about 5.30am and, after stabling the empty wagons after the close of work, I returned to Skipton with the light engines.

Work went well and good progress was made. On the fourth or fifth day, the snow clearance train had been placed in position, loading had commenced and at about 10.30 the sun came out like a summer's day. But soon the Helm Wind struck up and work was brought to a standstill When the staff trains arrived, the empty vehicles were propelled towards Blea Moor Tunnel on the up line and stabled for the day. With visibility down to almost nil, it was very difficult to get these trains back, loaded, and with the engines at the right end. Under such conditions, it was a miracle that there were no injuries, bearing in mind that men were rushing about in all directions, two-thirds of them being foreigners. The last of these trains departed about 7pm. Previously the empty wagon trains had been stabled overnight in a space we had cleared alongside the up home signal at Dent Head and under a steep embankment. To take precautions I decided to place the empty wagons over the viaducts on the up line towards the tunnel to prevent them being buried. We then had to concentrate on clearing the south side of Blea Moor tunnel. During these operations, as an experiment headquarters had obtained a jet engine from Rolls-Royce at Barnoldswick. This was placed on a flat wagon to see if it would blow the snow off the tracks. We spent several hours at Ribblehead one day before abandoning the idea, clearing only about 30yd as the hard-packed snow blew up in clumps, but I would like to have seen the engine's effect on fresh snow. It was about a fortnight before we go back to Dent Head. The sight ahead amazed us: looking towards Dent there was a sea of snow, the overbridges in Shale Cutting were out of sight and Dent Head's up home signal, which was on a 27ft post, had only about a yard sticking up out of the snow. However, the viaducts were fairly clear and the only good thing was that the wagons were almost free of snow. Trains commenced running as far as Ribblehead and work was resumed at Dent Head. On 18 March — six weeks after snow had first fallen in the area — a ground thaw set in and work could continue under greatly improved conditions. Every day we needed about a hundred new shovels from Leeds to replace those 'lost' by the POWs. I am sorry that I cannot recall exactly when normal working was resumed, but it was about the end of March 1947.

I must say that the whole of the staff worked wonderfully well in spite of frostbite, bloodshot eyes, peeling faces, colds and the lack of sleep. Many of them worked far and beyond the call of duty as was typical of railwaymen in that area.

Looking back, there is no doubt that the dieselisation of the Settle & Carlisle line made winter operations much easier. The performance of the diesel locomotives on heavy gradients is vastly superior to steam as they can maintain full power at all times. One instance of this is that half the signalboxes on the Long Drag have been closed since diesel traction was introduced, including Dent Head, Mallerstang and Ais Gill boxes. On the Long Drag, in either direction, steam locomotives were at their lowest ebb when they reached the 'danger area', where drifting was prevelant, and a few inches of snow was too much for them. This is why I always insisted that steam-hauled trains should be stopped at the earliest opportunity. On the other hand, despite not having seen diesels cope with ploughing snow on the Settle & Carlisle, I feel that the traction equipment might suffer from being blocked. As I noted above, Dent Head, Ais Gill and Mallerstang boxes have been closed. I always considered that the crossovers at the boxes were essential and cannot see how, when in conditions of heavy snowfall, ploughing could take place without them.

Below:
Ribblehead station on 23 March 1979. Batty Moss Viaduct in the left background
Terry Hanson

Steam past

Above:
The Midland Compounds were already in their twilight on the S&C when No 41140 was turned out to assist '4F' 0-6-0 No 43896 on a down mineral train near Lazonby on 22 May 1951. *R. Hewitt*

Below:
The '4Fs' continued to appear on the S&C almost until their withdrawal. No 44451 takes matters easily having been looped at Ais Gill signalbox with the southbound pick-up freight in July 1961. *Derek Cross*

Right:
By postwar days, the 'Patriot' 4-6-0s were rare performers on S&C line passenger trains. Aston's No 45550 was unusual power for the 8.35am Saturdays only Heads of Ayr-Leeds City seen near Kirkby Stephen on 29 July 1961. *D. Holmes*

Below:
A typical S&C express of the late 1950s. The 'Royal Scots' allocated to Holbeck never enjoyed a monopoly of Class '1' trains, and so the shed's 'Jubilees', such as No 45597 *Barbados*, were turned out. The 'Waverley' of 3 November 1959 was of its usual nine-coach formation (with LMS 12-wheel restaurant car) when it crossed Batty Moss Viaduct, Ribblehead.
Gavin Morrison

Above:
At the southern end of the line, there was an out and back Carlisle-Appleby stopping train, often headed by a Kingmoor '4' 2-6-4T, such as No 42313 approaching Armathwaite Viaduct with the 6.5pm to Appleby on 11 September 1961. *R. Leslie*

Centre left:
An uncommon sight on the S&C — one of the Stanier 2-6-0s. No 42977 is working a northbound goods upgrade to Blea Moor signalbox on 1 August 1964. *A. W. Martin*

Bottom left:
Doughty performers with express freight trains over the line were the 'Crab' 2-6-0s, such as No 42798 slogging uphill through Cumwhinton with a Carlisle-Leeds train on 6 April 1957.
R. Leslie

48454
APPLEBY WEST

Top left:
The taper boiler 2-6-4Ts appeared on the local trains to and from Garsdale. The afternoon southbound train passes Stainforth Sidings behind postwar No 42149 on 27 June 1961. *Derek Cross*

Bottom left:
The gruff voices of the Stanier '8F' 2-8-0s were well at home over the S&C. Snowplough-fitted No 48454 raises the echoes past Appleby goods shed with a southbound freight on 5 May 1967. *Derek Cross*

Top:
When the East Coast main line was severed by flooding north of the Border in 1948, the S&C was used as the diversionary route. At first sight, the pairing of '2' 4-4-0 No 40459 and LMS '5' 4-6-0 No 45223 is typical power for S&C route expresses, but in fact they are working the up 'Flying Scotsman' when photographed at Bell Busk (off the S&C line) in August 1948. *W. Hubert Foster*

Above:
The 'Jubilees' continued at work over the S&C line until the end of the 1967 summer season. No 45562 *Alberta* of Holbeck Shed has just cleared Batty Moss Viaduct with the summer Saturdays 06.40 Birmingham-Leeds-Glasgow of 19 August 1967. *Ken Hale*

Top right:
The rebuilt 'Royal Scots' put in some excellent work on the line, and usually looked smarter than No 46112 *Sherwood Forester* which was working the up 'Thames-Clyde Express' past Ormside, south of Appleby in July 1957.
P. Ransome-Wallis

Centre right:
Interesting performers over the S&C line in the late 1950s were Saltley's stoker-fitted '9F' 2-10-0s, diagrammed for the Water Orton-Carlisle Class 'C' out and return working. No 92167 is at grips with the 1 in 132 at Cotehill with the southbound train of 18 August 1959.
R. Leslie

Below:
The '9Fs' certainly were associated with the very last days of steam on the S&C, until Kingmoor shed lost its steam allocation at the end of 1967. This is the scene at Long Meg Sidings on 29 April 1967. No 92223 is approaching with empty hoppers, and No 92051 is ready to depart with a trainload of anhydrite. *Derek Cross*

Above:
Sections of constant uphill grade made the line ideal for controlled road testing of locomotives, and from 1924 onwards a number of unusual types were put through their paces. 'B1' 4-6-0 No 61353 drifts through Settle with a Carlisle-Skipton test train on 16 August 1951. *C. W. Bendall*

Below:
Rail tours, too, brought unaccustomed motive power over Ais Gill, such as 'Duchess' 4-6-2 No 46247 *City of Liverpool*, accelerating out of Hellifield with an RCTS tour of 9 July 1961 when the Pacific put up a rousing performance. *A. Robey*

Bottom:
As related by Peter Brock, the Gresley 'A3s' wrote a suitably proud final chapter to the story of steam (in normal working). No 60082 *Neil Gow* runs into Appleby with the afternoon Glasgow-Leeds express on 28 June 1961. *Derek Cross*

Steam finale over Ais Gill

Peter Brock

For 13 years after the Grouping of 1923, the former Midland Railway shed at Carlisle Durran Hill continued to operate independently of the main depots of Kingmoor and Upperby. Between them, the last two had absorbed the sheds of the G&SWR and Maryport and Carlisle at Currock Road, a mile south west of Citadel station. Durran Hill lay a mile to the south-east of the town, alongside the Midland main line from Carlisle to St Pancras, and was responsible for both freight and passenger train workings as far south as Leeds and Sheffield.

By the summer of 1936, it was found to be uneconomical for the LMS to have three separate depots in Carlisle, so Durran Hill was closed down and the staff and motive power divided up between the former LNWR shed at Upperby and the Caledonian shed at Kingmoor. Durran Hill shed lay deserted until the outbreak of World War 2 when it was taken over by the Army and used as a storage depot.

At Kingmoor, the daily rosters were separated into north and south links and the ex-Midland men continued to work trains over the Long Drag. The goods trains were worked on double lodging trips to Leeds with Derby '3F' and '4F' 0-6-0s. The top passenger turns included the 'Thames-Clyde' and 'Thames-Forth' expresses, the latter being the 10.05am from Edinburgh Waverley to St Pancras.

About 1936, Kingmoor shed was receiving new motive power in the form of the 'Jubilee' class '5XPs' which unassisted were able to take loads of 350 tons over Ais Gill. Trains in excess of this loading were provided with a pilot to Garsdale Junction where a turntable was provided for a comfortable return trip with the engine chimney-first. Turning on Garsdale's turntable could be difficult in stormy weather in view of the absence of a windbreak, and there was a case on record when Kingmoor '2P' 4-4-0 No 40602 spun round like a windmill for three hours before the Helm Wind dropped. This event took place in 1949. In the following spring, I started my railway service. I was too small for engine cleaning at first and was, as a result, employed as a booking-on clerk and, later, as a knocker-up. This duty consisted of waking up train crews at all hours during the night by knocking on their bedroom windows by means of a pole with a duster attached to its end. My transport was an official BR bicycle and always it seemed that I had to go to the most eerie places around the witching hour. I was chased by white owls, white ladies and fierce dogs.

So it was something of a relief to have reached the minimum height of 5ft 2in and be ready to take my firing test with Inspector Andrew Hughes. Andrew was an ex-Caledonian Railway driver who looked like an undertaker in his black overcoat and matching bowler, and he addressed all his underlings as 'laddie'. My test involved firing 'Black Five' 4-6-0 No 44958 to Carstairs on the 9.45am fully-fitted goods from Kingmoor down yard to Perth, made up to 44 fully laden vans. It was a Friday morning and the Perth driver was in a hurry to get home to collect his wages. The driver gave me and No 44958 a real flogging and I was taken off at Beattock after having allowed the water level to get dangerously low. I had failed my first main line test and had to continue on shed duties.

Eight weeks later I was given another trial, this time on 'Royal Scot' 4-6-0 No 46113 *Cameronian* working the 9.00am local passenger from Carlisle to Glasgow Central and loaded only to four coaches. I passed with flying colours, and at three months past my 17th birthday, my main line career had started. Only four days elapsed between passing the main line test and a baptism of fire on the Midland main line. I had booked on at 10.00pm at Kingmoor shed on Monday, 5 May 1952 as a spare passed cleaner. By 10.45pm, I was 'old hand' which meant that my senior colleagues had already been given firing turns, and I was next if anything turned up requiring an extra train crew. At 11.00pm, my lucky break came. The engine of the 9.50pm Glasgow St Enoch-St Pancras had stopped short of steam at Mauchline, Ayrshire, and the driver had requested assistance over the Long Drag from Carlisle to Garsdale.

The imposing chief shed foreman at Kingmoor, Harold Meekly, complete with frock coat and bowler hat, instructed me to accompany Senior Passed Fireman Isaac

Below:
The north end of Carlisle Kingmoor shed on 2 October 1966. Prominent is 'Jubilee' 4-6-0 No 45593 *Kolhapur* which had earlier worked a special, originating in Birmingham, over the Settle and Carlisle. A 'Britannia' and LMS '5' can be seen near the coaling plant. *David Birch*

Above:
A frequent motive power combination over the Settle & Carlisle in the absence of a Class '7'. LMS 4-6-0s Nos 44878 and 44775 take the 10.3am Edinburgh Waverley–St Pancras (later the 'Waverley') over Smardale Viaduct, 3 June 1952. *E. D. Bruton*

Left:
'Jubilee' 4-6-0 No 45715 *Invincible* crosses Batty Moss Viaduct with a relief to the down 'Thames-Clyde Express' on 17 August 1957. *A. Robey*

Below left:
'A3' 4-6-2 No 60092 *Fairway*, allocated to Holbeck shed, passes the former Durran Hill shed, Carlisle in July 1960 with the up 'Thames-Clyde' from Glasgow. Engine and men worked through to Leeds. *Peter Brock*

Norman to the stand-by road where LMS Compound 4-4-0 No 41135 stood patiently waiting an assignment. This old veteran of thousands of main line miles running looked well past her best, but still game for a few more encounters before departure to Valhalla. As I put the main line headlamps on the Compound, I wondered what she thought of me — a raw youngster on his first trip. If only she could have talked! My mate, Passed Fireman Ikey Norman, was already 53 years of age and was trying hard to get in his turns. In layman's terms, this meant that until he had completed 287 driving trips his basic pay would be that of a fireman. With the shortage of staff on the railways at that time I was soon to play a part in getting Ikey his final seven turns. However, that is another story. Our immediate task was to get down to the Citadel station and be in fine enough fettle to give the 'Midnight' a good pilot. We stood in the middle road of the station until the 9.50pm from St Enoch rolled in, 27 minutes late behind 'Jubilee' No 45711 *Courageous*. The load was 12

Above:
On the occasion described in the article, 'Royal Scot' 4-6-0 No 46129 *The Scottish Horse* heads the up 'Waverley' out of Carlisle. 'Kingmoor fireman Willie J. Cooke took the picture . . . I was too busy raking the cold fire . . .' *Peter Brock*

Right:
'A3' 4-6-2 No 60092 *Fairway* clears Blea Moor with the down 'Thames-Clyde' on 7 June 1960. An '8F' stands in the down loop. *P. A. Fry*

Below:
Neville Hill 'A3' 4-6-2 No 60086 *Gainsborough* is prepared at Holbeck shed to take the down 'Thames-Clyde' from Leeds on 14 March 1961. *G. W. Morrison*

Above:
Passed fireman Walter Tickner completes a brake test on 'A1' 4-6-2 No 60118 *Archibald Sturrock*, before working a special over the Settle & Carlisle line. One advantage of the 'A1s' compared with the 'A3s' was the independent steam brake which gave greater safety than the vacuum brake when steam pressure was low. *Peter Brock*

coaches including five heavy sleeping cars. The Glasgow Corkerhill crew told us that the '5XP' was a poor steamer and that they had hoped for something more substantial as a pilot than an old Compound. Otherwise they would have wired that their engine had failed altogether. I think No 41135 must have overheard this conversation because she drowned the rest of it by blowing off. We went forward to Carlisle No 5 box, then back on to the train. After tying-on and changing our lamps to express code we were ready for the 'off'. Station Inspector Jack Mumberson belled us out and Guard Tommy Bone of Scotby station gave us the green light from his handlamp. Ikey gave No 41135 a good handful of regulator in simple engine, and to the accompaniment of a few roars and slips from *Courageous* we vanished into the night past Cowan and Sheldons, the world-famous crane works. At this point, Ikey put No 41135's regulator fully over into compound working position and her exhaust beat altered to a three-cylinder syncopation.

The tender was loaded with the very best Yorkshire coal which began to show its worth in the first three miles of the trip as the Compound blew off steam as we passed Durran Hill South sidings. This optimistic note must have affected the '5XP' which also started blowing off when passing Scotby, a mile later. Both drivers decided to put the excess energy to good use and the sparks were soon flying. We passed the first summit of the southbound climb, at Low House Crossing (8.40 miles) in 14min and cleared Appleby (30.85 miles) in 37min from Carlisle. The long, gruelling ascent from Appleby to Ais Gill signalbox (17.55 miles) took 30min, but as I coupled off at Garsdale station I felt that we had put in a worthwhile night's work by helping the 'St Pancras' over a bad patch.

A few days after the trip with the Compound, I received a ticket from the BR messenger requesting me to report for duty at 9.30pm to work a special passenger train to Leeds. Arriving at Kingmoor shed and checking the daily board, I found that our engine was a Caprotti valve gear 'Black Five,' No 44755, and that the train was a military special from Glasgow St Enoch to Harwich Parkeston Quay. Isaac Norman was again my driver as he was senior 10pm relief man. As I topped up the water supply in the Caprotti's tender and then let the leather water-bag splash on to the sleepers, I wondered what sort of performance we could expect from this unusual 'Black Five'. The two-mile run past Bitts Park and Carlisle Brewery to Citadel station was like a ride in a Rolls-Royce wedding car and when our train arrived, 12 ex-LNER open thirds packed with boisterous Scottish troops and headed by 'Jubilee' No 45568 *Western Australia*, I thought we were in for a pleasant trip. This illusion was soon dispelled. As soon as we had passed Petteril Bridge Junction, only a mile from Citadel, we were down to 20mph. Isaac must have thought that my firing was at fault because he took over the shovel and put me behind the reverser which I dropped to no less than 35%. Isaac maintained the boiler pressure at 225lb all the way to Appleby, but despite his valiant efforts we took a full hour to cover the first 30 miles. There was a southbound freight standing at Appleby headed by LMS Mogul No 42905 and we effected a quick exchange. No 42905 managed to pass Ais Gill in the excellent time of 33min from Appleby. Isaac let the Mogul have her head over the tops past Blea Moor and we approached Settle Junction at around 70mph. There, a guard on the up road was waving his train inside with a red lamp and by mistake Isaac took the signal as an emergency and accordingly made a full brake application. Luckily, the offending guard realised his mistake and gave the 'all clear'. We arrived at Leeds City in 80min for 65 miles from passing Ais Gill box including the stop — not a bad night's work from an old Mogul!

An account of my firing over the Carlisle-Leeds road between 1952 and 1960 would fill many volumes, but in 1960, the 85th anniversary of the Midland Railway's entry into Carlisle, the finest hour of steam locomotive performance began. The 'XL limit' schedules of 1959 demanded that loads of 360 tons would be taken to Ais Gill in times almost equal to the immortal record set up by 'Jubilee' No 5660 *Rooke* on its 1937 test run. The 1959 schedules required almost a mile-a-minute timing over adverse gradients. The principal services affected by the new timings were the 12.05pm and 12.58pm departures from Carlisle, both St Pancras expresses. The 12.05 was the 'Thames-Clyde' express, the engine of which had the advantage of working through from Glasgow St Enoch. The 12.58, the 'Waverley', was a much tougher proposition from the fireman's point of view. He was at the mercy of the men of the Kingmoor preparing link who brought the engine down from the shed to the Citadel station. Some of the younger passed cleaners just filled up the firebox at the last minute and hoped for the best. This was no way to treat a '5XP', the type that invariably turned up even though the diagram clearly stipulated a 'Royal Scot'. The shortfall was the result of Leeds Holbeck shed substituting the engine of the Bradford stock/parcels train with anything they could lay their hands on. So Kingmoor was left holding the baby when this train arrived at Carlisle without a 'Scot'.

As a junior fireman it was no surprise that the selection of train crews for the first week of the fast (arguably impossible) timings between Carlisle and Leeds included Kingmoor's 'speed merchants': Brigham Young and 21-stone heavyweight Bass Telford. Bass was a little hard of hearing and found he could drive engines best by their exhaust note, a technique which was very unfortunate for the fireman's welfare! The next piece of misfortune for the rest of the Midland link at Kingmoor was the combination of Brigham and Bass as the drivers of Kingmoor 'Jubilees' Nos 45713/14 *Renown* and *Revenge* at the head of the up 'Waverley' on 11 February 1959. They demonstrated that the timings could be kept and managed to pass Helwith Bridge at a full 95mph, for which each received appropriate action from the authorities. By their exploit they showed the Control Office that the timings were not quite impossible. The problem of the timings lay in strategy more than anything else. It was easier to drop a few minutes to Armathwaite and then make a fast sprint to the first stop at Appleby rather than empty the boiler on this first section, wind the locomotive and be unable to fight back. The schedule for the 30.85 miles to Appleby was 34min start to stop, with 24min allowed for the savage 17½-mile haul to Ais Gill summit.

In June 1959, I was in the spare link at Kingmoor and booked with a wonderful young driver called Pat Moran. We were both delighted when booked to do a contract week's work on the up 'Waverley'. Pat liked his dominoes and darts, but when I discussed the challenge of 'timing' the 12.58 he said that if I could put them in, he could put them out. We tried for the full week with 'Jubilees' No 45696 *Arethusa*, No 45691 *Orion*, No 45716 *Swiftsure*, No 45704 *Leviathan* and No 45697 *Achilles*. But with the best will in the world we were unable to pass Ais Gill on time.

From the summer of 1959 until the spring of 1960 I was promoted to the regular north goods link, as a result of the health problems of one of the regular firemen. I had the great fortune to be the regular fireman of undoubtedly the fastest driver of Kingmoor, the one and only Randall Scott. Randall was to perish in a terrible accident at Eastriggs in 1975 when a heavy lorry overturned, crashed through the overbridge and plunged on to the main line right in front of the 'Northern Irishman' express. Randall was driving an English Electric Class 40 and his fireman, Jackie Farrow, also lost his life in the disaster.

The spring and early summer of 1960 brought a new and magnificent contender to solve the difficulties confronting train crews on the Leeds-Carlisle-Glasgow workings. These saviours were a batch of ex-LNER 'A3' Pacifics transferred to Holbeck from East Coast main line duties. The 'A3s' had been improved to give their finest performances — ironically in their last days — by Mr K. J. Cook, the great Swindon engineer who had been transferred from the hallowed GWR works to Doncaster Plant. I was soon to find out the reserve of power at the command of an 'A3' Pacific when I fired for Randall on the up 'Waverley' on 6 April 1960. Our engine was No 60038 *Firdaussi*. From the start, it was evident that the 'A3' had the capacity to handle the 12-coach train with ease. However, I shall never forget the sight of Randall being thrown from the driver's seat and landing among the coal when *Firdaussi* went into a traditional Gresley slip at Howe & Co's Sidings. This fault apart, the 'A3s' were master of the Settle & Carlisle. It all depended on how much coal could be delivered to the voracious firebox, although in return the 'A3' would knock spots off the demanding schedules.

At all the ex-LMS depots (Holbeck, Kingmoor and Corkerhill) involved with the 'A3s', the general impression was that although dirty engines to work on, their splendid capacity for steaming covered a multitude of sins. In midsummer 1960, Randall Scott and I enjoyed a number of runs with 'A3s' over the Midland main line. On 27 July 1960, we were booked to work a Butlin's holiday special from Glasgow to Filey and decided to test the maximum performance of an 'A3' over the Settle & Carlisle. Our engine was No 60093 *Coronach*, loaned to Kingmoor by Carlisle Canal. The load was eight ex-LNER coaches — well within *Coronach's* ability to maintain 'XL' timings on the Midland road. Randall worked the 'A3' at around 35% cut-off all the way to Armathwaite (10.00 miles) passed in 15min. Another quarter of an hour saw us past Appleby and when we passed Ais Gill box in 16min flat from Appleby (17½ miles) we knew that we had beaten *Rooke's* record of 1937. However, the 'A3' had a significant advantage in boiler capacity over the '5XP' which size for size was still the victor.

Two days later we were able to compare a 'Royal Scot' against No 60093's performance. We had No 46129 *The Scottish Horse* on the up 'Waverley' as far as Hellifield. We were able to equal *Coronach's* time exactly as far as Long Marton, but the booked stop at Appleby put an end to any further comparison.

When the LNER Pacifics were discussed in the bothies at Corkerhill, Kingmoor and Holbeck, one variety stood head and shoulders above the rest in popularity: this was the Peppercorn 'A1' class. The general consensus was that they were easier to prepare than a 'Royal Scot' and gave a smoother ride, yet the drivers were very cautious about hitting high speeds in view of the alarming rolling and lurching of the 'A1s', especially on the downhill run from Ais Gill to Carlisle. I was lucky to have No 60133 *Pommern* for the heaviest firing turn I ever experienced with a passenger train over the Midland main line. This was the 6.30pm St Enoch-Eastbourne car-sleeper. With a load of 18 vehicles we were able to reach Engine Shed Junction, Leeds (112 miles) in only 140min from Durran Hill. The arrival of the 'A1s' on the Midland line represented the high-water mark of steam but they were soon superseded by the BR/Sulzer Type 4 diesels.

As a footnote to the work of the LNER Pacifics on the Leeds-Carlisle line, the signalman at Mallerstang box told we that they were the only engines able to clear the section to Ais Gill in the same time as the diesels. Enough said!

Below:
No 60118 makes a fine sight as it passes Petteril Bridge Junction with an S&C line train in 1963. *Peter Brock*

Main line steam revival

British Rail
runs out of steam
Last steam train makes
historic special farewell journey
Sunday August 11th
Liverpool/Manchester
to Carlisle & back
This will be the very last train to operate on standard gauge track headed by a B.R. steam locomotive. 314 nostalgic miles, 10¾ happy hours, with luncheon, high tea, other refreshments, souvenir ticket and souvenir scroll. 15 guineas.
Liverpool Lime Street Dep 09.10–Arr 19.50
Manchester Victoria Dep 11.06–Arr 18.48
For Tickets. Write quickly to Passenger Marketing Manager, British Rail, London Midland Region, Euston House, London NW1. Mark your envelope Personal and enclose £15.15 per ticket required. Money immediately refunded if the 470 seats have already been sold.
British Rail

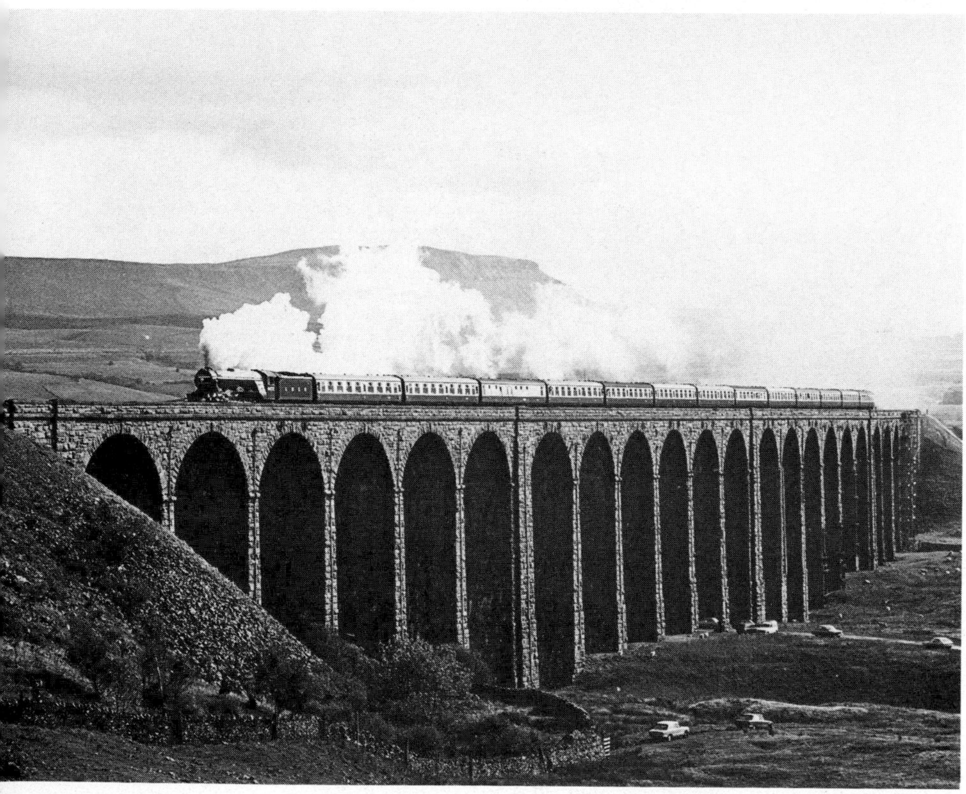

The Settle & Carlisle line saw the 'last' steam train run by BR, an enthusiasts' excursion on Sunday, 11 August 1968. Ten years later, in March 1978, main line steam was back, with excursions run by the Steam Locomotive Operators' Association. From 1980, the 'Cumbrian Mountain Expresses' (or 'Pullmans') have been operated, some sponsored by SLOA, some by BR

Above left:
The poster for BR's 'last' steam train.
David C. Hall

Above:
'Britannia' 4-6-2 No 70013 *Oliver Cromwell* arrives at Ais Gill with the last steam train, 11 August 1968. *T. A. Heyes*

Left:
***Flying Scotsman* has frequently worked over the S&C since 1978. One of its most important workings was the 'Lord Bishop', the Euston-Appleby/Armathwaite excursion, to the memorial service for Eric Treacy held at Appleby on 30 September 1978. No 4472 is seen northbound on Batty Moss Viaduct that day.** *A. R. Kaye*

Above:
The LMS '5' 4-6-0s are particularly suited to the character of the line. No 5407 displays its defiance of the 1 in 100 gradient as it fights up to Blea Moor with the 'Cumbrian Mountain' of 17 August 1983. *W. A. Sharman*

Left:
Dent station looks cared for as 'K1' 2-6-0 No 2005 passes with the 'Northumbrian Mountain Pullman' of 20 March 1983, which it worked Hellifield-Carlisle-Newcastle-Middlesbrough. *John S. Whiteley*

Below left:
The splendid pairing of Midland Compound No 1000 and 'Jubilee' No 5690 *Leander* on the southbound 'Cumbrian Mountain Pullman' of 12 February 1983. *Tim Grimshaw*

Top right:
'West Country' 4-6-2 No 34092 *City of Wells* storms towards Blea Moor signalbox with the northbound 'Cumbrian Mountain Pullman' of 30 April 1983. Note that the loops were both still in situ. *John Titlow*

Centre right:
Crowdundle Viaduct, between New Biggin and Long Marton, is crossed by SR 4-6-0 No 850 *Lord Nelson* with the southbound 'CME' of 14 September 1983. *Brian Dobbs*

Bottom right:
***Duchess of Hamilton* will now forever be associated with the S&C, although members of its class never regularly worked over the line. This photograph shows all the ingredients of the magnificent spectacle: the distinctive outline of Pen-y-Ghent, the 'Duchess' resplendent in maroon with a dramatic exhaust and, behind the engine, the LNWR Royal Train Brake and two umber and cream National Railway Museum Pullmans. The northbound 'CME' was photographed at Selside on 29 October 1983.** *Dr John Sagar*

34092

CUMBRIAN
MOUNTAIN
EXPRESS
850
272

Inspector George Gordon, Carlisle

Michael Harris

To those who knew it in steam days Carlisle had a magnetism, excitement even, which today's West Coast electrification and general rationalisation have largely removed. That is not to say that the city's railway interest has gone, nor indeed would one deny that train operations are any less efficiently handled than in the past. But the sight of main line steam locomotives standing at either end of Citadel station waiting to take over incoming trains was one of the special sights at Carlisle. With it went a railway tradition that spanned several pre-grouping companies, the LMS and the LNER, and, of course, generations of railwaymen.

Steam died at Carlisle at the very end of 1967 when Kingmoor shed lost its allocation for good. The West Coast electrification came in 1974 and probably no one imagined that a main line steam locomotive would ever again work a train into Carlisle. The Settle & Carlisle line's centenary was celebrated in 1976, but steam did not make its reappearance over the Long Drag and into the Border City. When it did, it was on the chill and snow-swept Easter Saturday, 25 March 1978. At the head of the 'Norfolkman' charter train, from Euston via Leeds and the S&C, LNER 'V2' 2-6-2 No 4771 *Green Arrow* made a triumphant entry into Carlisle. No 4771 worked back south from Carlisle with another 'Norfolkman' charter train on 27 March and so began the St Martin's Summer of steam over the Settle & Carlisle route. The Traction Inspector who ensured that the 'V2's' debut was a successful one was George Gordon. Since then, he and a number of enthusiastic railwaymen based at Carlisle have worked hard over the last four seasons to recreate that sight of a main line steam locomotive standing proudly at the end of Citadel's platforms ready to take over an express train.

A local man, George Gordon started his railway career at Kingmoor shed during 1935, but with the unhappy, post-Depression condition of those days, found himself redundant by October. However, he was reinstated the following March, to work at Kingmoor until 1939 when he transferred to

Right:
Inspector Gordon in the cab of *Lord Nelson*, 29 July 1981. *David Eatwell*

Left:
Carlisle Upperby, 8 March 1980. LMS '5' No 5305 waits for its 'Cumbrian Mountain Express' duty on a trip when Inspector Gordon was on the footplate to 'advise, encourage and supervise'. *Peter J. C. Skelton*

Below left:
Inspector Gordon was on the footplate of LMS 'Duchess' No 46229 *Duchess of Hamilton* as it approached Ais Gill with the southbound 'CME' of 8 November 1980. Driver J. Lister and Fireman D. Smith were the crew.
Graham Wignall

Kirkby in Ashfield shed. From there, he worked on freight trains over the gruelling Derby-Manchester via Peak Forest route and to Wellingborough and also got to know all the colliery sidings in the Nottingham area. This was before entering military service with the Royal Engineers at Longmoor in October 1939. But the LMS was short of firemen and so George went back to railway service, *twice*, as it happens. Wartime work was arduous, what with blackout tarpaulins making footplate work a dirtier and sweatier business than usual, but in George's words, 'that was the time when railwaymen really had to have their hearts in their work... departments worked very closely with each other... it was a great experience for enginemen'. He recalls that he was booked to a locomotive which hauled Monty south before D-day.

George Gordon was promoted to outside running shift fireman at Kingmoor in 1958. The job was a challenge. It involved co-ordinating the work of men on the shed — those disposing of locomotives, fire-droppers and other shed workers. Central to the job was getting engines off shed *on time* for their trains. With an awkwardly placed turntable, only the most careful planning and supervision ensured that 50 locomotives went on and off shed in the busiest shift, between 10pm and 6am. His next move was to the former LNER shed at Carlisle Canal in 1961, as a higher grade foreman. Then to Upperby, a well-arranged depot with good facilities, but sadly, it was being run down, in the face of dieselisation. Now George moved away from sheds, to become a running inspector at Carlisle. That time included being in charge when the last passenger train left Silloth, in October 1964. It was an occasion not to be forgotten. Before departure, someone attached the train to a capstan at Silloth docks and on the journey to Carlisle the communication cord was pulled repeatedly. There was another day when he was again master of ceremonies, this time when the last DMU departed Keswick for Penrith. The decline of the network in the Carlisle area was offset by modernisation on the main line, but one thing *seemed* clear: Inspector Gordon could not imagine that he would deal with steam traction again.

This short biography, outlining the career of one man and spanning the developments in British railway history during a period of change, has so far neglected one dimension. George has a real interest in railways. He comes from a family, perhaps like many others in Carlisle, whose life has centred on railways. His father was a driver for 47 years, he has three uncles on the railway and three of the members of his family have given a total of 147 years service. George has two more years at work before retirement. One can't help wondering whether the devotion to duty on railways by families will continue, or will go with the last vestiges of the old order. Certainly, today's railway service is very different. There are fewer people employed and many will say that the old camaraderie is hard to sustain in the face of single-manning on locomotives, intensive diagramming and the reduction in the number of depots.

But to return to present-day steam working. George Gordon has again become a master of ceremonies, not on a 'last' train but with the supervision of locomotives working the 'Cumbrian Mountain Express' or on charter trains running to or from Carlisle. The footplatemen are in charge of the locomotive, but the inspector is there to advise, encourage and supervise. Unlike ordinary timetable trains, there is always a margin of judgement, given the fact that steam workings today require decisions on handling, at water-stops and in the liaison between locomotive owners, footplatemen and operators. George recalls that much of the spirit of working and learning together came from the Mutual Improvement Classes, that remarkable movement that represented so much of the spirit of devotion to duty by enginemen. One area for judgement concerns counselling drivers and firemen to avoid generating black smoke, or blowing off unnecessarily. Such care was always part of good enginemanship but today's environment is even less tolerant of smoking chimneys and ear-piercing safety valves.

As at Carnforth, Carlisle has recreated a steam department within today's modern railway. The main difference, of course, is that there is no steam centre at hand. Upperby steam shed has been transformed into a modern carriage servicing depot, and main line steam locomotives working out of Carlisle are stabled and serviced there, by courtesy of the Area Maintenance Engineer. Any mention of Carlisle brings to mind the name of Michael Carrier, Assistant Area Manager, Carlisle, who has expended tremendous effort in the cause of steam, particularly in arranging for the coaling of locomotives at London Road coal depot, disposal and preparation facilities at Upperby (there is still an ash-pit there) and general train running arrangements for 'Cumbrian Mountain' and other workings over the S&C between Carlisle and Dent. Michael Carrier has been involved in liaison with the C&W department at Upperby and, certainly, friendly and constructive assistance is synonymous with the Upperby staff who are also involved in the maintenance of SLOA's Pullman car set based at the depot. However, apart from the personnel accompanying the visiting private locomotive, it is the driver booked to work the train who is responsible for seeing that his charge is ready for the road. Talking of enginemen, there are nine drivers and 12 firemen volunteers at Carlisle. Of these, two of the firemen are members of the Carlisle Railway Society, a good case of enthusiastic railwaymen, rather than enthusiast railwaymen perhaps.

We were talking about good enginemanship before and it was interesting to hear George's comments about locomotive handling. The difficulties fall into two main areas — a boiler too full of water, or too heavy a fire. In the second case, George diagnoses the fault as 'enthusiasm' for the shovel: some firemen returned to the art are so concerned about being blamed for subsequent shortage of steam that they build up a big fire which won't then burn through fast enough, with the result that boiler pressure drops ominously. Stop-watching and tape recording enthusiasts like fast starts, not least from Appleby on the southbound 'Cumbrian Mountain Express', but George warns that too vigorous a start to Griseburn portents trouble on the last stages of the climb to Ais Gill.

For locomotives starting cold out of Carlisle, the immediate prospect is daunting. The climb, largely at 1 in 132, south from Petteril Bridge Jn up to beyond Cotehill is a severe test with a 450/500-ton load. It is worth remembering that in steam days, apart from wartime years, such heavy passenger trains were seldom worked with a single locomotive over the Settle & Carlisle. Look at photographs of S&C route trains in the latter years of steam working and you will be lucky to see anything over nine coaches unpiloted. Today, apart from well-loaded trains, the crews may face a locomotive completely foreign to them. There have been scarcely any 'duff' runs, but George Gordon comments that despite some fine performances the appearance of *Lord Nelson* on a train promises heavy shovelling. Once again, the Gresley locomotives come in for praise, particularly once Carlisle men had altered their firing technique to suit the LNER saucer-fire principle. Not that some of the steam panel at Carlisle are unused to Gresley motive power, as the group is made up from men formerly at Canal shed, as well as ex-Upperby.

That serves as an introduction to the run I enjoyed with the 'Cumbrian Mountain Express' of 19 August 1981. On a chilly, wet morning 'A3' 4-6-2 No 4472 *Flying Scotsman* was standing over the pit at Upperby, attended to by Steamtown staff and other local well-wishers. For this run Richard Hardy was the VIP footplate rider and having travelled north with No 4472 on the 'Cumbrian Coast Express' from Carnforth-Sellafield the day before, he was full of praise for her general condition. In due course, the BR crew arrived, Driver K. Tubbs and Fireman J. Day. They would work Carlisle-Appleby. From Appleby, the crew was Driver J. Lister and Fireman G. Routledge who provided a rather special link with the past. For J. Lister had been the driver on that memorable last train from Silloth back in 1964 when his mount was Ivatt '4' 2-6-0 No 43139. The Silloth branch was worked by Canal shed and it followed that Lister had regularly fired, and driven Gresley Pacifics over the Waverley Route. So, yet again, the main line steam of today reflected a special part of the traditions and memories of the past.

Driver Lister's expertise ensured that No 4472 was nicely 'on beat'. With a little poetic licence, despite or because of the appalling weather, it was not difficult to imagine that the 'Cumbrian Mountain Express' had transferred temporarily to the erstwhile Waverley Route. Largely worked at 35% cut-off and full regulator, No 4472 made an excellent climb with its 12-coach, 460-ton train from the Appleby restart to Ais Gill, passed in 29min 38sec. In a steady drizzle, Driver Lister made an excellent slip-free departure from Appleby. With 50mph before Ormside, 33½ at Griseburn, 47 after Crosby Garrett, we were past Kirkby Stephen (10.65 miles) in 18min 02sec. The engine slipped slightly in Birkett Tunnel, but from a minimum of 31½mph beyond, took advantage of the ease in gradient past Mallerstang to make nearly 40mph and finally plugged away at a steady 35-36mph up to Ais Gill. The rest, of course, was easy but on a filthy day with lashing rain and a strong cross-wind the climb from Appleby was a tribute to No 4472, her crew and George Gordon. Maybe that VIP footplate rider had somethig to do with it, too!

From Skipton, the Carnforth crew with 'A4' 4-6-2 No 4498 *Sir Nigel Gresley* put in some good work, particularly after Clapham, and despite checks, engine and men made their home town on time. As George Gordon says, the volunteer steam crews are out to make a good job of it.

I have left to the end George Gordon's shock admission. 'Marvellous away from starts Gresley Pacifics,' he said, 'perhaps I shouldn't tell you, but a couple of years ago I was (jokingly!) sent to Coventry for saying that an LNER 4-6-2 was better than a 'Duchess' over the Settle and Carlisle!'

Left:
There's a magic about this shot of 'A3' 4-6-2 No 4472 *Flying Scotsman* near Birkett Tunnel with the 'CME' of 19 August 1981, the run described in the article. *L. A. Nixon*

Moods

Above:
Tranquility — a view towards Kirkby Stephen with 'Jubilee' 4-6-0 No 45697 *Achilles* on a down train, near Birkett Tunnel, July 1965.
W. J. V. Anderson

Left:
Typical S&C weather — a strongish wind is blowing a steady downpour. This was Dent station on 13 April 1964 with LMS '5' 4-6-0 No 45201 on the 11.58am Hellifield-Carlisle stopping train. *D. Holmes*

S&C snowscape. Drifting represented the worst enemy of the operators, but the great hills under a covering of snow look magnificent.

Above:
BR/Sulzer 1-Co-Co-1 No 61 at Dent Head Viaduct with the morning Leeds-Glasgow express on 2 March 1974. The northern portal of Blea Moor Tunnel may be seen left.
J. H. Cooper-Smith

Left:
Class 25 Bo-Bo diesel electric No 25.142 with an oil tank train on the chilly morning of 27 April 1981. There had been a notable blizzard three days earlier. The train is heading south from Grisedale Crossing, near Garsdale.
T. G. Flinders

Above right:
Duchess of Hamilton **approaches Ormside Viaduct with the southbound 'CME' of 11 February 1984. The River Eden is in the foreground.** *W. A. Sharman*

Right:
The undramatic northern start of the S&C, surrounded by pylons and housing estates. A LMS '5' 4-6-0 faces the start of the 1 in 132 climb from Petteril Bridge Junction, Carlisle past Scotby on 30 May 1967. *P. Cotterell*

The summer 1959 timetables

Bell Busk Station is closed. The locality is served by omnibuses operated by the Ribble Motor Services and Pennine Way.
For complete service between Leeds City, Bradford Forster Square, Keighley, Ilkley and Skipton, see North Eastern Region tables.

§—Passengers change at Lancaster Green Ayre and is Second class only from that point.
†—Passengers change at Morecambe Promenade and is Second class only from that point.
A—On Saturdays departs Manchester Victoria dep. 3.38 p.m.
C—On Saturday mornings arrives Carlisle 5.5 a.m.
D—Sunday to Friday nights.
E—On Saturdays arrives Glasgow St. Enoch 10.28 p.m.
F—On Saturdays arrives Newcastleton 5.42 a.m., Hawick 6.22 a.m., St. Boswells 6.43 a.m., Melrose 6.54 a.m., Galashields 7.0 a.m., Edinburgh Waverley 7.57 a.m.
G—Glasgow Central, and on Saturdays arrives 6.22 p.m.
H—Monday to Friday nights.
J—Glasgow Central.
K—Applies 29th August, 5th and 12th September only.
L—On Saturdays arrives Hawick 5.1 p.m., Melrose 5.45 p.m., Galashiels 5.51 p.m.
N—On Saturdays arrives Edinburgh Waverley 7.10 p.m.
P—Edinburgh Princes Street.
Q—On Saturdays arrives Lancaster Green Ayre 11.4 p.m. depart 11.6 p.m. Heysham arrive 11.20 p.m.
R—Edinburgh Princes Street and applies Fridays only. On Saturdays arrives Edinburgh Princes St. 8.23 p.m.
T—Passengers change at Lancaster Green Ayre.
V—On Saturdays arrives Hawick 9.1 p.m.
X—Saturday nights.
FO—Fridays only.
RC—Restaurant Car.
RB—Buffet Car.
SC—First and Second Class Sleeping accommodation.
SO—Saturdays only.
SX—Saturdays excepted.
TC—Through Carriage.

a—a.m.
b—On Saturdays departs Leeds City 5.20 p.m.
c—On Saturdays arrives Skipton 9.51 a.m.
d—On Saturdays arrives Skipton 11.52 a.m.
e—One minute later on Saturdays.

GARSDALE AND HAWES

The Passenger Train Service between Garsdale (for Hawes) and Hawes has been withdrawn and Hawes station is closed. The locality is served by omnibuses operated by the Ribble Motor Services Ltd.

BRITISH RAILWAYS

Right:
Extracts from the BR London Midland Region public timetable of 15 June-13 September 1959.

Table 218 SKIPTON TO MORECAM[BE]

WEEKDAYS

Miles	Station		No.												
				a.m.	FO p.m.		SO a.m.	SX a.m.	FO p.m.	p.m.	p.m.	a.m.	a.m.	a.m.	
	180 LONDON St. Pancras	dep.	1		7 55				8 50	9D0	9D15				
					SO a.m.				SO a.m.	a.m.	a.m.				
	LEEDS CITY	"	2	1 15	1 43					2 17	2 57	4 5		6 3	
	BRADFORD Forster Square	"	3				1 35	2 0				4 20			
	KEIGHLEY	"	4	1 46			1 56	2 21			3 28	4 58		6 37	
	ILKLEY	"	5												
0	**SKIPTON**	arr.	6	1 58			2 9	2 34		2 52		5 11		7 2	
		dep.	7	2 4						2 59				7 5	
3¾	Gargrave		8											7 13	
6¾	Bell Busk		9												
10	**HELLIFIELD**	arr.	10	2 21					3 0	3 15				7 29	
—	143 MANCHESTER Victoria	dep.	11												
—	**HELLIFIELD**	dep.	12	2 23					3 5	3 18				7 35	
11¼	Long Preston		13											7 38	
15	Giggleswick		14											7 46	
20¾	Clapham		15											7 59	
25	Bentham		16											8 8	
28¼	**Wennington**	arr.	17											8 15	
		dep.	18											8 20	8 30
34¾	Caton		19											8 32	
36¼	Halton		20												
38¾	**LANCASTER Green Ayre**	arr.	21											8 40	
39¼	164 LANCASTER Castle	arr.	22											8 55	
	0 **LANCASTER Green Ayre**	dep.	23											8 44	
39¼	½ 164 Scale Hall	arr.	24											9§ 2	
42¼	— **MORECAMBE PROMENADE**	arr.	25											8 52	
45¼	7¼ **HEYSHAM**	"	26											9†54	
31	Arkholme (for Kirkby Lonsdale)		27												8 37
34½	Borwick		28												8 45
37¾	**CARNFORTH**	arr.	29	3 10											8 52
15¼	Settle		30												
21¼	Horton-in-Ribblesdale		31												
26	Ribblehead		32												
32¼	Dent		33												
35¼	Garsdale (for Hawes)	arr.	34												
	Do.	dep.	35												
45¼	Kirkby Stephen West		36												
56	**Appleby West**	arr.	37							♣4 16					
		dep.	38							4 18			7 34		
59	Long Marton		39										7 39		
62	New Biggin		40										7 45		
63½	Culgaith		41										7 49		
67	Langwathby		42										7 56		
68¼	Little Salkeld		43										8 0		
71½	Lazonby & Kirkoswald		44										8 5		
76¾	Armathwaite		45										8 14		
86¾	**CARLISLE**	arr.	46		4 15				4 47	4C52	5 30		8 31		
202¼	241 GLASGOW St. Enoch	arr.	47		7 55				7 31		8 30		2 28		
132¾	HAWICK	"	48							6F13			10 42		
147¾	MELROSE	"	49							6F47			11 26		
151¾	GALASHIELS	"	50							6F53			11 32		
184¾	EDINBURGH Waverley	"	51							7F52			12 27		

- FO p.m. 7 55 / SO a.m. 1 43 column: Runs 27th June to 1st August inclusive. T.C. London St. Pancras to Glasgow St. Enoch
- FO p.m. 8 50 column: Runs until 5th September inclusive. T.C. London St. Pancras to Glasgow St. Enoch
- p.m. 9D0 column: S.C. and T.C. London St. Pancras to Edinburgh Waverley. Does not convey Edinburgh Sleeping Car Passengers from London St. Pancras. ♣Also calls at Newcastleton arr. 5F33 a.m. and St. Boswells arr. 6F34 a.m.
- p.m. 9D15 column: S.C. and T.C. London St. Pancras to Glasgow St. Enoch.
- a.m. 8 20 column: T.C. Leeds City to Morecambe Promenade
- 8 30 column: T.C. Leeds City to Carnforth.

WEEKDAYS—*continued*

Station		No.														
			a.m.	SO p.m.	SO p.m.	SX p.m.	p.m.		SO p.m.	p.m.	p.m.	SO p.m.	SX a.m.	SO a.m.		SX p.m
180 LONDON St. Pancras	dep.	1											9 15	9 15		
													p.m.	p.m.		
LEEDS CITY	"	2	11 45	12 17			12 15			12b032	12 45	1 20	1 46	1 58		1 53
BRADFORD Forster Square	"	3	12 10		12 43					12 50	1e10					1 40
KEIGHLEY	"	4	12 34	12 47	1 2						1e34	1 50				2 23
ILKLEY	"	5					12 58			1 22						
			p.m.													
SKIPTON	arr.	6	12 51	12 59	1 14		1 20			1 44	1e51	2 2	2 18	2 31		2 37
	dep.	7			1 16	1 16			1 36				2 20	2 34		2 40
Gargrave		8				1 25			1 45							
Bell Busk		9														
HELLIFIELD	arr.	10			1 32	1 42			2 2				2 35	2 50		2 57
143 MANCHESTER Victoria	dep.	11							11 48					12 30		
HELLIFIELD	dep.	12			1 33	1 50			2 10				2 38	2 52		2 59
Long Preston		13				1 53			2 13							
Giggleswick		14														
Clapham		15			1 50											3 18
Bentham		16														3 27
Wennington	arr.	17														3 34
	dep.	18													3 39	3
Caton		19														
Halton		20														
LANCASTER Green Ayre	arr.	21			2 13											4
164 LANCASTER Castle	arr.	22			2 22											4
LANCASTER Green Ayre	dep.	23			2 15											4
164 Scale Hall	arr.	24			2§32											4
MORECAMBE PROMENADE	arr.	25			2 25											4
HEYSHAM	"	26			3†24											4†
Arkholme (for Kirkby Lonsdale)		27													3 44	
Borwick		28													3 52	
CARNFORTH	arr.	29													3 59	
Settle		30				2 2			2 22							
Horton-in-Ribblesdale		31				2 15			2 35							
Ribblehead		32				2 29			2 47							
Dent		33				2 41			2 59							
Garsdale (for Hawes)	arr.	34				2 48			3 6							
Do.	dep.	35														
Kirkby Stephen West		36														
Appleby West	arr.	37											3 33	3 50		
	dep.	38											3 35	3 52		
Long Marton		39														
New Biggin		40														
Culgaith		41														
Langwathby		42														
Little Salkeld		43														
Lazonby & Kirkoswald		44														
Armathwaite		45														
CARLISLE	arr.	46											4 14	4 25		
241 GLASGOW St. Enoch	arr.	47														
HAWICK	"	48											5 24	5 43		
MELROSE	"	49											5 54	6 14		
GALASHIELS	"	50											6 0	6 20		
EDINBURGH Waverley	"	51											6 53	7 17		

- SO p.m. 1 14 column: T.C. Bradford Forster Square to Morecambe Promenade
- SX a.m. 9 15 column: THE WAVERLEY R.C. and T.C. London St. Pancras to Edinburgh Waverley. Also calls at St. Boswells arr. 5.41 p.m.
- SO a.m. 9 15 column: THE WAVERLEY R.C. and T.C. London St. Pancras to Edinburgh Waverley. Also calls at St. Boswells arr. 6.4 p.m.
- 3 39 column: T.C. Leeds City to Carnforth
- SX p.m. column: T.C. Leeds City to

…ND CARLISLE

WEEKDAYS—*continued*

a.m.	a.m.	SO a.m.		SO a.m.	a.m.	SX a.m.	a.m.	SO a.m.	SX a.m.	SO a.m.	SO a.m.		SO a.m.	SO a.m.	a.m.	SO a.m.	a.m.	SO a.m.	SX a.m.	SO a.m.	SO a.m.	a.m.	a.m.	SO a.m.	SX a.m.		SO a.m.	a.m.	SO a.m.	SO p.m.	SO p.m.	
																			4 20	4 20												1
8 10					8 40		8 47	9 5	9 10	9 23			9 43				9 45	10 20	10 35	10 35				10 47	10 47		11 0		11 14			2
	8 10	8 30		8 35	8SX47	8 30	9 10	9 35			9 40				9 50		10 10					10 43						11 10				3
8 42		8 53		8 59	9 21	9 2	9 34	9 55	9 41		10 4			10 21			10 34		11 1	11 1		11 6		11 16	11 16		11 31	11 34	11 47			4
	8 42														10 22																12 25	5
8 54	9 4	9 6		9 16	9 34	9 24	9c48	Runs 11th July to 22nd August inclusive.	9 58		10 18			10 34	10 44		10 51	11 0	11 15	11 15		11 23		11 29	11 29		11 47	11d51	noon 12 0		12 47	6
		9 10			9 36	9 40					10 20			10 36				11 2	11 19	11 19	11 22			11 38	11 38		11 52		12 2	12 22	12 53	7
						9 48															11 29									12 30		8
																																9
		9 27			9 53	10 4								10 53		10 59		11 18	11 35	11 35	11 44			11 58	11 58		12 9		12 19	12 46		10
																9 20		9K20	9 20												T.C. 9.40 a.m. from Saltburn, 10.7 a.m. from West Hartlepool to Blackpool Central arr. 2.8 p.m. (Table 153) T.C. 9.40 a.m. Saltburn to Southport arr. 3.5 p.m. (Table 153)	11
		9 28			9 55	10 7							Runs 25th July to 29th August inclusive.	10 55		11 3		11 23	11 37	11 37	11 46		11 55	12 1	12 1		12 14		12 24	12 48		12
						10 10															11 49		11 58	12 4	12 4					12 51		13
						10 18					Commences 11th July.			Runs 11th July to 29th August inclusive.		T.C. 9.20 a.m. Manchester Victoria to Glasgow Central		R.C. Leeds City to Kilmarnock T.C. Leeds City to Glasgow St. Enoch	R.C. Leeds City to Kilmarnock T.C. Leeds City to Glasgow St. Enoch	T.C. 7.58 a.m. Derby Midland to Glasgow St. Enoch. Table 180.	11 56			12 11	12 11					12 59		14
						10 31															12 7			12 22	12 22					1 12		15
		9 55				10 39															12 15			12 30	12 30		12 42			1 20		16
		10 0	10 8			10 46															12 21			12 36	12 36		12 49		12 58	1 27		17
						10 47															12 22			12 38	12 43	12 48	12 51		1 3	1 29		18
						10 56															12 31					12 57				1 41		19
						11 1															12 36					1 2				1 46		20
		10 14			10 34	11 7					11 14			11 34							12 42					1 8	1 5			1 55		21
		10 22			10 52	11 22					11 22			11 52							12 52					1 22	1 22		T.C. Leeds City to Windermere arr. 2.47 p.m. 11th July to 29th August inclusive. Table 51			22
		10 16			10 36	11 8					11 16			11 36							12 43					1 10	1 7			1 56		23
		10§32			11§ 2	11§32					11§32			12§ 2							1§ 2					1§32	1§32			2§ 2		24
		10 24			10 44	11 16				11 0	11 24		11 31	11 44							12 51					1 18	1 15			2 4		25
		10†52				12† 1				12† 1	12† 1		12† 1	12† 1							1†23					1†34				2†22		26
										T.C. 7.50 a.m. Sheffield Midland to Morecambe Promenade. Table 180				T.C. 5.50 a.m. Nottingham Midland to Morecambe Promenade Table 180										12 43	12 48							27
			10 34																					12 51	12 56							28
																								1 3	1 3							29
		T.C. Bradford Forster Square to Morecambe Promenade	T.C. Bradford Forster Square to Carnforth.		T.C. Leeds City to Morecambe Promenade	T.C. Bradford Forster Square to Morecambe Promenade SX		T.C. Leeds City to Gourock arr. 3.35 p.m.			T.C. Bradford Forster Square to Morecambe Promenade		T.C. Leeds City to Morecambe Promenade			Runs until 22nd August inclusive							12 7	T.C. Leeds City to Carnforth	T.C. Leeds City to Carnforth	T.C. Leeds City to Morecambe Promenade	T.C. Leeds City to Morecambe Promenade					30
																							12 20									31
																							12 32									32
																							12 44						T.C. Leeds City to Barrow-in-Furness arr. 2.31 p.m. Table 163		Runs 11th July to 15th August inclusive	33
																							12 51									34
																							12 52									35
																							1 5									36
																12 6		12 21	12 35	12 35			1 17									37
																12 8		12 23	12 37	12 37			1 19									38
																							1 24									39
																							1 30									40
																							1 34									41
																							1 41									42
																							1 45									43
																							1 50									44
																							1 59									45
								12 5								12 52		1 11	1 11	1 34			2 13						Runs 4th July to 29th August inclusive.			46
																3J40		3 53	3 53	4 19			6G10									47
																		3 14	2 55				4L53									48
																		3 47	3 26				5L28									49
																		3 53	3 32				5L34									50
																		4 48	4 34	4P 6			6N52									51

WEEKDAYS—*continued*

SO p.m.		SO a.m.	p.m.	a.m.	SO p.m.	p.m.	p.m.		p.m.	p.m.	p.m.	SX p.m.	SX p.m.	SO p.m.	SX p.m.		p.m.	p.m.	p.m.	p.m.		p.m.	p.m.	p.m.		p.m.	FO p.m.	SO p.m.	SX p.m.	p.m.	p.m.	p.m.
		9 20		10 15								12 15		12 15												2 15		3 15	3 15			5 5
1 53		p.m.		p.m. 2 46		2 45	3 14			3 45	4 18	4 55		4 55			5SX8	5 12	5b15	5 42			5 45	6 47		7 45	8 2	8 35	8 35	8 45	9 25	10 10
1 45			2 10			3 10			3 40	4 10	4 40		5 10				5 20		5 40			5 53	6 10	7 10		8 10	8 35			9 10		10 45
2 29			2 34			3 34	3 45		4 6	4 34	5 4	5 20		5 27			5 45		6 4	6 17			6 34	7 34		8 34	8 58	9 3	9 6	9 34	9 54	11 9
					3 0													5 52				6 25										
2 41		Runs 27th June to 29th August inclusive	2 51		3 22	3 51	3 57		4 26	4 51	5 21	5 32	5 37	5 39			6 5	6 14	6 21	6 40		6 47	6 51	7 51		8 51	9 11	9 24	9 26	9 51	10 6	11 26
2 44							4 4		4 28			5 42		5 50	5 50					6 43							9 16	9 28	9 31		10 10	
							4 12							5 57	5 57					6 51							Runs 17th July to 21st August inclusive	9 36	9 38			
3 1							4 28		4 43			6 0		6 12	6 12					7 7								9 52	9 53		10 26	
							12 45													4A37								6 30				
3 3				THE THAMES—CLYDE EXPRESS R.C. and T.C. London St. Pancras to Glasgow St. Enoch			4 33		5 5			6 2		6 14	6 14					7 10								9 56			10 28	
							4 36		5 8					6 17	6 17					7 13								9 59				
							4 44							6 24	6 24					7 21								10 7			T.C. Leeds City to Heysham	
3 22							4 58							6 35	6 35					7 34								10 20				
3 31							5 6							6 43	6 43					7 42								10 28				
3 38							5 13							6 49	6 49					7 49								10 35				
3 43	3 50						5 18	5 23						6 50	6 50					7 54	8 0							10 36				
							5 33							6 59	6 59					8 3												
							5 38		T.C. Bradford Forster Square to Carlisle																		T.C. Bradford Forster Square to Heysham.					
	4 8						5 44					6 38		7 7	7 7					8 11								10 52			11Q6	
	4 22						5 52					6 52		7 22	7 22					8 22								11 22			11 22	
	4 10						5 46					6 40		7 9	7 9					8 13								10 53			11Q8	
	4§32						6§ 2					7§ 2		7§32	7§32					8§32								11§ 2				
	4 18						5 54					6 50		7 17	7 17					8 21								11 1			11§36	
	4†54													8† 4	8† 4					8†59							10 23	11T18			11Q32	
3 48								5 28																								
3 56								5 36																								
4 3								5 44													8 19											
T.C. Leeds City to Carnforth	T.C. Leeds City to Morecambe Promenade	T.C. London St. Pancras to Glasgow St. Enoch.					T.C. Leeds City to Morecambe Promenade	T.C. Leeds City to Carnforth	5 17			T.C. Leeds City and Bradford Forster Square to Morecambe Promenade		T.C. Leeds City to Morecambe Promenade						T.C. Leeds City to Morecambe Promenade	T.C. Leeds City to Carnforth						In connection with Belfast Steamer Sailings.	T.C. Leeds City to Morecambe Promenade	T.C. Leeds City to Hellifield		In connection with Belfast sailings, Steamer departs Heysham about 11.55 p.m. (SX) and about 12.40 a.m. Sunday and arrives Belfast about 7.0 a.m. (MX) and about 8.0 a.m. (Sunday)	
									5 30																							
									5 42																							
									5 54																							
									6 1																							
									6 3																							
									6 16																							
									6 28																							
									6 32																							
									6 37																							
									6 43																							
									6 47																							
									6 54																							
									6 58																							
									7 4																							
									7 13																							
		4 50		5 9					7 29																							
		7 30		7 55					10E42																							
				7V45					10SO44																							
				9 34																												
				9 40																												
				7R57					10P 5																							

Below:
The River Ribble at Helwith Bridge. The change in gradient hereabouts is clearly seen as 'West Country' 4-6-2 No 34092 *City of Wells* does battle with the Long Drag at the head of the northbound 'CME' of 3 December 1983.
W. A. Sharman